THE
HEALING JOURNEY

THE
HEALING
JOURNEY

Your Journal of Self-Discovery

PHIL RICH, EdD, MSW

STUART A. COPANS, MD

John Wiley & Sons, Inc.

NEW YORK • CHICHESTER • WEINHEIM • BRISBANE • SINGAPORE • TORONTO

This publication is designed to provide accurate and authoritative information in regard to the subject matter covered. It is sold with the understanding that the publisher is not engaged in rendering professional services. If
professional advice or other expert assistance is required, the services of a
competent professional person should be sought.

Library of Congress Cataloging-in-Publication Data:
Rich, Phil.
    The healing journey : your journal of self-discovery / by Phil Rich,
Stuart A. Copans.
       p.   cm.
   ISBN 0-471-24712-X (pbk. : alk. paper)
   1. Diaries—Therapeutic use. 2. Psychotherapy—Problems,
exercises, etc. I. Copans, Stuart. II. Title.
RC489.D5R53   1998
616.89'14—dc21   97-28988
                                       CIP

Printed in the United States of America.
10 9 8 7 6 5 4 3 2 1

CONTENTS

Embarking on the Path to Healing

Why Keep a Journal?

As you walk down the path to healing, you may experience intense emotions, flashes of insight, and periods of loneliness and sorrow. Your journal can be a valuable companion on the road to growth and self-discovery.

Your journal provides a place for you to express your thoughts, feelings, ideas, questions, and concerns as you feel them. You can write down your innermost thoughts, explore them, and later go back and reexamine, rethink, or just plain remember them. In your journal you can talk with and be honest with yourself, in a way that is perhaps difficult under other circumstances. And your journal allows you to get in touch with parts of yourself that are hidden. Your journal can be another voice for you.

Make journal writing an important part of your life. You can write in your journal as the day proceeds or set aside time each day to write in your journal.

When and How to Use Your Journal

If you take your journal writing seriously, setting aside time to write will become important. As you become more comfortable with journal writing, you may find that you only need to write in your journal when you feel like it, rather than every day. We recommend that you write daily, however, and thus become more self-reflective and better able to process how you feel, without shutting off the feeling or being overwhelmed by it.

Consider using your journal before a planned meeting, or if you are in a relationship with a therapist, an individual, or a group in which it is important to become increasingly self-aware and raise issues for discussion and further exploration in the relationship. It may help you to decide the issues you'd like to talk about in the meeting, or simply organize your feelings and thoughts. In any situation where self-awareness and self-expression are important, writing in your journal before the meeting or session will help clarify feelings and thoughts. Writing in your journal shortly before a therapy session is a good way to guarantee almost immediate support for any issues that may come up in your writing.

Consider using your journal after an important meeting, group, or therapy session to help you remember the issues raised in the interaction, as well as to provide you with a tool for recognizing, processing, and expressing your feelings and thoughts. Writing in your journal shortly after a therapy session is a good way to help you to make more sense of the session, and to keep the therapy fresh and alive.

Organization

Most of the exercises in *The Healing Journey* are independent of one another and can be completed in any order. If you are working with a therapist or group leader, he or she may assign a journal exercise. If you are working on your own, you must decide where you should start.

The Healing Journey contains 40 different journal exercises that all follow the same format:

- An overview of the exercise
- Instructions for completing the exercise
- A sample exercise (in some cases)
- The exercise itself, with room to record your answers
- Process Points—things to think about as you record your responses or process them with a therapist

These exercises can be completed in any order, but they have been grouped together in five major sections and are generally best completed in that sequence. These sections are:

Section I *Learning to Speak to Yourself*   This section contains exercises that are designed to help you get comfortable with the journaling process.

Section II *Looking in the Mirror*   The exercises in this section all share the basic theme of getting to know your inner self a little better. They will help you explore your thoughts, feelings, and personality.

Section III *Seeing Yourself in the World*   The exercises in this section are primarily intended to help you see the world outside of yourself from a different perspective.

Section IV *Recording Your History*   There are many ways to document, record, and reflect on your past and present. The exercises in this section focus on the journal as a diary of events, memories, and feelings.

Section V *Charting Your Future: Finding Solutions and Solving Problems*   These exercises develop your ability to think about how you think; they will help you change your approach to solving problems and making decisions about your life and future.

At the end of each section are Section Reviews. Similar to the Process Points found at the end of each individual exercise, they provide you with a way to look back at, review, and process your experience with each section as you complete it.

Although most people find it easiest to start with Exercise 1 and work through the rest in sequence, you may elect to begin elsewhere. Read through all of the exercises to familiarize yourself with *The Healing Journey* before beginning your trip.

Beginning Your Journey

Regardless of the exercise with which you start, you'll have to decide for yourself how emotionally comfortable you are with journal writing, and you'll have to decide for yourself when, how, and where to journal write. Some people like privacy, others prefer writing in a public area.

Here are some suggestions that might help you decide where and what is best for you to write as you begin your journal. If you think that journal writing may be emotionally difficult for you, take special note of the items on the list that address your emotional comfort and safety as well as your physical comfort.

- Do some relaxation exercises before you begin, to get your mind and body both working and relaxed.
- Take breaks during your writing if you need to. Stretching your legs can also give your mind a break.
- Consider playing some quiet music or other relaxing sounds in the background.
- Make sure you have pens, pencils, coloring pens, or other writing/drawing instruments that are comfortable for you to use as you write.
- Pick a place to write that will be physically comfortable for you.
- Pick a place to write that will be emotionally comfortable and safe for you. It might be an area that is quiet and private or one that is busy and public.
- Make sure that people are nearby if you think that your journal writing may become overwhelming.
- If writing is emotionally difficult for you or you find your feelings or ideas overwhelming at times, consider having a comforting picture or object nearby, or something else that you find familiar and safe.

Once you've completed an exercise, reread what you've written. Simply writing things down and never processing them is not very useful. Discovery and exploration are not stagnant. Your journal is intended to be a *working* tool in your journey of self-exploration and healing.

As we have said, this workbook is primarily intended to help the journaling process as a tool for personal exploration or self-help, and/or for those engaged in therapy. We believe, then, that some of our readers will be in some sort of psychotherapeutic relationship, and we want to encourage those readers to use their journal *in conjunction with* their therapy and to share its contents with their therapists. In these cases, a journal can serve as an important addition to therapy. It offers the opportunity to add later thoughts and explore issues that come up in or out of therapy in greater detail, with the luxury of time and without the pressure of responding immediately. Your journal offers both you and your therapist greater insights into yourself and also allows your therapist to gain insight that can be shared with you through an analysis of *how* you write, *what* you write about, what you *don't* write about, and how you express yourself.

Whether you are currently working with a therapist or starting on the path to discovery on your own, above all remember that your journal is just that—*your* journal. It is written *by* you, *for* you. Don't be influenced by the fact that you may allow someone else to later read what you have written. Write your journal for yourself and not someone else who may later read it. Be honest in what you write!

If you use it regularly and honestly and reread and reflect on what you've written, your journal can be an integral part of your journey toward healing. Indeed, you may come to enjoy the journal growth process so much that you will embrace it as part of your daily routine long after the pages of this original workbook are filled.

THE
HEALING
JOURNEY

Learning to
Speak to Yourself

A Promise to Myself

Overview

This first exercise will immediately encourage you to think about the whole point of this book. It reflects the goals of journaling and the underlying principles on which successful journal writing and self-discovery and growth are built.

 This journal represents a major investment of your time and energy. As in any relationship—with people, with objects, or with institutions—what you gain from the relationship is likely to match what you put into it. At the end of each section in *The Healing Journey,* you will have a chance to consider what you have learned, what you have gained, and whether to renew your commitment.

Instructions

It is healthy to begin with a period of exploration before making a significant commitment. Read through this exercise, and then complete Exercise 2. Then come back and sign this commitment. Think about each of the promises you're being asked to make. Read them, think about them, and sign this "contract" with yourself.

THE EXERCISE

1. I promise to use this journal as another voice for my innermost feelings and thoughts, and as a tool for emotional and personal growth.
2. I promise to read this journal regularly.
3. I promise to be honest with myself in this journal.
4. I promise to write this journal for *myself*—not for anyone else who may later read it.
5. I promise to stay committed to this journal and to my journey toward healing.

YOUR SIGNATURE _____ DATE _____

PROCESS POINTS

- Have you ever been really honest with yourself? Is the idea of honesty scary? Does knowing this journal is for you, and you alone, make it less scary?

- How do you decide to commit to something? Do you commit too quickly, then resent your commitment and break it off? Are you so afraid of making a mistake that you avoid making any commitment at all?

EXERCISE  2

Thinking about Your Journal

Overview

This exercise is intended to help you think about your journal. What do you want from it, and why? How and when are you likely to use it, and to what ends? Under what conditions is it easiest for you to write in your journal? This exercise provides you with the opportunity to think about the process and uses of journaling, and the chance to commit yourself to using a journal.

Instructions

As you answer these questions, please think about them. Don't just answer yes or no or give the answer you think others may want to hear. There are no "right" answers.

The idea is for you to think about the value of journal writing to *you,* and about how you can best get going. So please give explanations with your answers. Think about the meaning of the questions.

THE EXERCISE

DAY: _____   DATE: _____

1. Do you think that journal writing might be useful to you?

   _____

   _____

   _____

   _____

2. If you already keep a journal, are you satisfied with the way you currently use your journal? Is it a satisfying and productive experience?

   _____

   _____

   _____

   _____

3. Will you generally make one journal entry a day or more than one entry a day?

_____

_____

_____

_____

4. Are you likely to let other people read your journal?

_____

_____

_____

_____

5. Whom will you consider allowing to read your journal?

_____

_____

_____

_____

6. Will allowing others to read your journal affect what you write?

_____

_____

_____

_____

7. Where will you be the most emotionally comfortable and safe while writing? Where will you write?

_____

_____

_____

_____

8. Does it make sense to write shortly *before* important meetings with therapists or work groups that you regularly attend?

_____

_____

_____

_____

9. Does it make sense to write shortly *after* other important meetings you regularly attend?

_____

_____

_____

_____

10. What kind of meetings do you regularly attend—therapy sessions, group meetings, work groups, committee meetings, others?

_____

_____

_____

_____

11. Do you need people nearby when you finish writing so that you can connect with others?

_____

_____

_____

_____

12. Will stretching or breathing exercises before you write help get your mind and body working?

_____

_____

_____

_____

13. What favorite or comfortable things will you want to have around as you write?

_____

_____

_____

_____

14. What favorite music or relaxing sounds might help as you write?

_____

_____

_____

_____

15. What are some other ways that you can stay safe and comfortable while you're journal writing?

_____

_____

_____

_____

16. What other thoughts do you have about journaling?

_____

_____

_____

_____

_____

_____

_____

_____

PROCESS POINTS

- If you gave very brief or one-word answers, are you really committed to keeping this journal?

- Are you ready to work on your own growth and healing?

- Did you list someone you'd feel comfortable letting read your journal? Will that person be available emotionally to help support you in your journaling?

EXERCISE  3
Guided Writing

Overview

Guided writing is a simple, structured way to help you start journaling, if you get a little stuck. Guided writing provides you with starting points and requires you to write about predetermined subjects. To this degree, guided writing shapes what you will write about and the order in which you will respond. It can be a great tool for getting started.

Instructions

Each sentence begins with what we call a *sentence start,* which is just that—a way to start a sentence and get your thoughts running. As you complete the following sentences, write intuitively, using all of the words or thoughts that enter your mind. Don't edit yourself; just go with it.

THE EXERCISE

DAY: _____   DATE: _____

I'm the kind of person who _____

_____

I feel close to people who _____

_____

My journal is _____

_____

Other people think I _____

_____

I would like to let other people know that _____

_____

I'm my own worst critic because _____

_____

I'm my own greatest strength because _____

_____

Right now I feel _____

_____

I'd rather be _____

_____

Complete these sentences in more detail.

1. When I think of what I want in life and what I actually have, I feel . . .

_____

_____

_____

_____

_____

_____

2. I would like other people to know that . . .

_____

_____

_____

_____

_____

_____

3. I have never been able to forget that . . .

_____

_____

_____

_____

_____

_____

4. I find my life to be . . .

_____

_____

_____

_____

_____

_____

Think of five sentence starts of your own and complete each of them in two different ways.

1. Sentence start: _____

    a. _____

    _____

    _____

    _____

    b. _____

    _____

    _____

    _____

2. Sentence start: _____

    a. _____

    _____

    _____

    _____

    b, _____

    _____

    _____

    _____

3. Sentence start: _____

   a. _____

   _____

   _____

   _____

   b. _____

   _____

   _____

   _____

4. Sentence start: _____

   a. _____

   _____

   _____

   _____

   b. _____

   _____

   _____

   _____

5. Sentence start: _____

   a. _____

   _____

   _____

   _____

   b. _____

   _____

   _____

   _____

PROCESS POINTS

- Was it easier to come up with sentence starts for yourself or to have them provided for you? What does this teach you about your approach to writing and self-reflection?

- Did having sentence starts provided for you hinder or help your creativity and self-exploration?

- Do you need some format, structure, or person to prompt you on your journey of self-discovery?

EXERCISE 4

Structured Writing

Overview

Structured writing is like the guided writing we showed you in Exercise 3—it's just a little more structured (hence the title). It's another way to help you start journal writing when you feel stuck, and it builds on the basic idea of guided writing and sentence starts. A primary difference between guided and structured writing is that structured writing is more than a series of basically unrelated sentences and thoughts. It provides more of a process for further developing your thoughts or ideas in a sequential manner, with each structure building directly on the idea before it.

Instructions

Plan to write for 15 to 30 minutes. Pick your subject matter and develop your thoughts. After that, just fill in the blanks.

THE EXERCISE

DAY: _____   DATE: _____

TIME STARTED: _____   TIME ENDED: _____

1. What three things about my life are on my mind right now?

    • _____

    • _____

    • _____

2. Which of these three things do I want to explore in writing right now?

    _____

3. I want to write about this part of my life because . . .

    _____

    _____

    _____

    _____

    _____

4.   This part of my life makes me feel . . .

_____

_____

_____

_____

_____

5.   This part of my life has an important effect on me because . . .

_____

_____

_____

_____

_____

6.   I wonder if I can ever change this aspect of my life because . . .

_____

_____

_____

_____

_____

7.   This part of my life frightens me because . . .

_____

_____

_____

_____

_____

8.   Writing about this makes me feel . . .

_____

_____

_____

_____

_____

9.   Now I need to . . .

_____

_____

_____

_____

_____

Instructions

You must read what you write in your journal if it is to have real value to you. Take a moment to read again what you've just written, and then think about it for about 5 minutes *without writing*. Then write down any new thoughts that you may have about what you've written, or clarify your thoughts further in writing.

Now, after 5 minutes of thought, answer this question. *Right now, I feel:*

PROCESS POINTS

- Do you ever stop long enough in your daily routine to actually think about your life and what's weighing on your mind at that moment? What is it like to reflect on your life in this way?

- Of the three things you said were on your mind, how did you choose the topic you actually wrote about?

- Was it useful to be assisted in your thinking by structured questions? Why?

Associations

Overview

This is a "clustering" exercise to stimulate your ideas and thinking and provide another way to loosen up your journal writing and explore your thoughts and feelings. It is called *associations* because its major purpose is to help you build on your ideas, associate other ideas with that central idea or theme, and recognize patterns in your thinking and writing process.

Instructions

Use a single word or a brief phrase you want to build on; think of an idea that you want to explore and build on; or just use the first word or phrase that comes to mind. As a topic, choose:

- The first word that comes to your mind
- The way you are feeling right now
- The way you would like to feel
- A memory that easily comes to mind
- A word that describes someone important in your life
- The way you feel about the world today
- An image in your mind or imagination
- Anything you want

However, once you have committed this word or phrase to paper, the rest of the exercise involves using the first words or brief phrases that come to mind—you may not edit your thoughts or ideas.

1. Write your word or brief phrase somewhere on the blank page and circle it.

2. This is a free-association exercise. Somewhere above, below, before, or after your first word write down a second word that comes to mind *as a result of* the first word you wrote. Then draw a connecting line between the words, with an arrow indicating the direction. That is, the arrow should point from your first word toward your second. You have just made an association, even if it's not clear why.

3. Now briefly reflect on what that second word means to you, and write in a third word somewhere. The third word can be above, below, before, or after

your second word and should be connected directly to the second word by a line and an arrow showing the direction.

4. Keep going this way until you run out of connecting ideas and associations.

5. Go back to your original word and go through the process again, developing a new line of association.

6. As you move through your second, third, and more set of associations, you can choose to move off that new connecting line and across to a set of connecting lines that you have already developed and add to it, or spin off a brand-new line from an existing word.

7. Stop when the page gets too complex, or when you plain run out of juice.

8. Now look at what you've done and let the associations come together in your mind. Think about what the sets of associations you've created might mean to you, or how they make you feel. Write an entry of no more than 5 to 10 minutes that reflects on the meaning of what you've done, how it makes you feel, or what you are thinking now. This entry should help you add meaning to the set of associations you've created or realized.

Here, we provide an example for you of what a series of associations looks like. This web of associated words is often referred to as a "cluster" of ideas, thoughts, and feelings.

THE EXERCISE

DAY: _____   DATE: _____

1. Draw your association web (the "cluster").

2. What meaning does this web have for you? Take 5 to 10 minutes and write about its meaning, using step 8 from the Instructions as a guide.

_____

_____

_____

_____

_____

_____

_____

_____

_____

_____

_____

_____

_____

_____

_____

_____

_____

_____

_____

_____

_____

_____

_____

_____

_____

_____

_____

_____

_____

_____

_____

_____

PROCESS POINTS

- Why did you select the particular word or topic you did as the starting point for your web? How central is that idea in your life and why?

- As you created your web, did you feel more like the fly (the victim), the spider (the producer), or both?

- In what way is your life like a web of clustered themes and relationships? Can you extricate yourself from the web of your life; do you want to?

Self-Questions

Overview

Self-questions provide yet another way to get unstuck when you are keeping a journal. They provide you with a jumping-off point, or a subject about which to write. Self-questions can be written as sentence starts such as "I like myself because . . ." or as open-ended questions such as "Why do I like myself?" Depending on how they are worded, some self-questions can help you to *feel* out your answers and others can help you to *think* out your answers.

Instructions

The instructions are minimal. Think about some questions you'd like to ask yourself, and write them down. You can pick from the list of sample questions below, or you can make up your own. Remember that your self-questions can be in the form of sentence starts or open-ended questions.

Write down at least five self-questions, and then write your answer to each question until you feel you're done. Spend at least 5 minutes on each answer. If you find that you can't spend 5 minutes or more on each answer, write about why you can't.

Examples of Self-Questions

What is important to me?

- What do I want from my friends?
- What do I want from my family?
- What do I want from my lover?
- What do I want from myself?
- On what do I place value?

What motivates me?

- What do I do for others?
- What do I do for myself?
- What do others do for me?
- What do I want others to do for me?

What is my identity?

- Who am I?
- Do I know who I am?
- What do I reveal of myself to others?
- What do others know of me?

- Who have I been?
- Who will I become?

Where am I going?

- Where have I been?
- Where do I want to go?
- Where can I go?
- What can I do to get where I want to go?
- Do I know where I'm heading?

THE EXERCISE

DAY: _____ DATE: _____

Question 1: _What is important to me? = What makes me happy_
Where am I going
What do I want to accomplish
Or what do I place value

Answer 1: _To be a good mother to Rob_
— Teach him to be good person
— "   "   to succeed + be happy

→ _'. To be happy myself — for which I need_
1) Good relationship w/ Richard
2) Friends / family who love + respect me
3) To feel I've contributed to making the world better
4) To accomplish something each day - either
a) productive work, b) recreation/time w/ others
c) fun play [need to elaborate each of these]
5) To be in a beautiful place
6) To be in shape - get regular exercise + eat well
7) To laugh + be silly
8) To be in touch with the transcendent -
my God =

Question 2: _____

_____

_____

_____

Answer 2: _____

_____

_____

_____

_____

_____

_____

_____

_____

_____

_____

_____

_____

_____

_____

_____

_____

_____

_____

Question 3: _____

_____

_____

_____

Answer 3: _____

_____

_____

_____

_____

_____

_____

_____

_____

_____

_____

_____

_____

_____

_____

_____

_____

_____

Question 4: _____

_____

_____

_____

Answer 4: _____

_____

_____

_____

_____

_____

_____

_____

_____

_____

_____

_____

_____

_____

_____

_____

_____

_____

_____

_____

_____

Question 5: _____

_____

_____

_____

Answer 5: _____

_____

_____

_____

_____

_____

_____

_____

_____

_____

_____

_____

_____

_____

_____

_____

_____

_____

_____

Instructions

If you keep a list of self-questions to answer or explore, you'll always have a place to start writing if you get stuck with your journaling. Questions might reflect points or issues from individual or group therapy sessions, ideas to ponder, things people have said, or ideas you've read.

Use the following space to list more self-questions you might be interested in exploring later.

_____

_____

_____

_____

_____

_____

_____

_____

_____

_____

_____

_____

_____

_____

_____

_____

_____

_____

_____

_____

PROCESS POINTS

- Coming up with answers can be very difficult, but did you find it more difficult or easier to come up with self-questions in the first place? Do you know yourself well enough to pose the right questions you'd like to answer?

- Was it difficult to answer the questions you asked? Why?

- Which self-questions required you to feel out your answers and which required you to think them out? Do you recognize a difference between feeling and thinking? Which did you find more useful to the journaling process and why?

Questioning the Question

Overview

A subquestion results from the answer to an earlier or "originating" question. Creating subquestions resembles the process that children might go through when they ask why the sky is blue, and on hearing that the sky is blue because of the ozone layer, might ask why there is an ozone layer. As many parents or others who spend any time around young children may know, one answer leads to another question.

Instructions

Start with a question that is important to you. Answer the question. At the end of your answer look for another, related question—then answer that second question. Repeat this process until you have exhausted all possible subquestions or you run out of steam, but generate at least five subquestions.

1. Ask yourself a question that you would like to explore. It can be anything: "Is there meaning to life?" "Should I buy a new refrigerator?" "Why am I so unhappy?" "What do I want most out of my life?" "Am I happy with my relationships?"

2. Explore your answer in writing. Write your question in one color ink and your answer in another. Or underline your question. Do something to make the question stand out.

3. After you've written the answer to your main question, think of another related question (question 1*a*) that follows logically from the answer to your first question. Write it down on the next line. Explore subquestion 1*a,* ponder your answer, and write it down.

4. Go to a third subquestion (question 1*b*), and so on. Keep going until you've exhausted the subject, answered your own original question to your satisfaction, or otherwise feel you've completed your exploration for the moment. Remember, the point here is to explore your own thoughts and ideas, and to get to know yourself a little better.

Example

QUESTION 1: *Why am I afraid to share my journal with my spouse?*
ANSWER 1: Because it contains my private thoughts.
SUBQUESTION 1*a*: *Why don't I want to share my private thoughts with my spouse?*
ANSWER 1*a*: Because I'll feel vulnerable.

SUBQUESTION 1*b*: *Why will I feel vulnerable with my spouse?*
ANSWER 1*b*: Because I can't trust my spouse.
SUBQUESTION 1*c*: *Can I trust anyone?*
ANSWER 1*c*: No.
SUBQUESTION 1*d*: *Why can't I trust anyone?*
ETC.

THE EXERCISE

This worksheet allows you one originating question and five subquestions, but you can continue on for as long as you like. It is simply intended to help you get started.

DAY: _____ DATE: _____

Primary question 1: _____

_____

Answer to question 1: _____

_____

_____

_____

_____

_____

Subquestion 1*a:* _____

_____

Your answer to 1*a:* _____

_____

_____

_____

_____

_____

_____

Subquestion 1*b:* _____

_____

Your answer to 1*b:* _____

_____

_____

_____

_____

_____

Subquestion 1*c:* _____

_____

Your answer to 1*c:* _____

_____

_____

_____

_____

_____

Subquestion 1*d:* _____

_____

Your answer to 1*d:* _____

_____

_____

_____

_____

_____

Subquestion 1*e:* _____

_____

Your answer to 1*e:* _____

_____

_____

_____

_____

_____

_____

PROCESS POINTS

- Did this exercise help you reach a more significant level of understanding about the originating question?

- Did your final subanswer leave still more questions to be asked or lead to other avenues of questioning? Why did you stop there? Did you feel you had completely answered the originating question?

- What questions—stemming from your original question—are still to be asked (and answered)? Are you prepared to keep journaling for the answer? If not, why not?

Stream of Consciousness

Overview

Stream-of-consciousness writing simply means that you start with an idea—any idea—and ramble. Let your pen (or mind) take you where it wants to go. Don't worry about coherence or making sense. Don't worry about finishing sentences. Don't worry about legibility. Go with the ideas as they come up. Simply write what's in your mind at that exact moment, even if you wind up repeating yourself. Try to be free enough to let your mind wander from one idea to the next, without restriction. Sometimes, this kind of approach is referred to as *free-form* writing, *freestyle* writing," or *automatic* writing.

Instructions

For this exercise, set aside 5 to 10 minutes and write. Don't lift your pen or pencil off the paper. If you have to keep repeating the same thought over and over, that's okay. Whatever you do, keep writing—and let your mind wander where it will!

THE EXERCISE

DAY: _____   DATE: _____

Suggestion for a starting point: What are you thinking about or feeling right now?

_____

_____

_____

_____

_____

_____

_____

_____

_____

_____

_____

_____

_____

_____

_____

_____

_____

_____

_____

_____

_____

_____

_____

_____

_____

_____

_____

_____

PROCESS POINTS

- Are you finding the exercises more difficult or easier as they become less structured?

- Are you finding that you require or seek more or less structure in the journaling exercises? Do your needs for more or less structure in the exercises reflect a need for a similar level of structure in your daily life?

- Did the stream-of-consciousness exercise raise issues or feelings you need to spend more time addressing or resolving?

Fridge Poetry

Overview

This technique is named after the magnet refrigerator poetry that has become popular recently. Fridge poetry, in case you haven't seen it, consists of a series of individual words that magnetically stick to a refrigerator. You can take any of the words and rearrange them in any order to make a sentence, spell out a message, or make a poem—all from found materials (in this case, the individual magnetized words that are available to you). It can be a great way to get creative with only what is available to you.

Of course, you don't have to buy a set of magnetic words to be a refrigerator poet. You can simply make up your own set of words or cut words out of a magazine—but the trick is to do so *at random,* without consciously selecting the words. From these words—these found materials—you can be creative and make poetry.

Instructions

Randomly cut out 100 words from a magazine (or elsewhere). From these, pick individual words and create a poem that describes how you feel right now, an idea you have, the way you see things at the moment, a memory—or anything else you'd like to explore about yourself through these found words.

There are many ways to create this poem; you select the ground rules. Your poem can have rhyming sentences, it can be limited to a certain number of sentences (anywhere from one to as many as you can create out of 100 words) or to no more than a certain number of words in each sentence, and so on. But the original 100 words must be selected at random, and you must describe the ground rules of your poem (such as the number of sentences in the poem), *before* you actually create it.

Reproduce your poem in the space provided.

Then reflect on the poem. How does reading it make you feel? What does the poem tell you about yourself? What meaning do you find in the way that you have rearranged an otherwise random and meaningless series of words?

THE EXERCISE

1. Before you create your poem, what ground rules, if any, have you decided on?

_____

_____

2. Why have you picked these ground rules?

_____

_____

_____

_____

3. Reproduce your poem in the space provided.

_____

_____

_____

_____

_____

_____

_____

_____

_____

_____

_____

_____

_____

_____

_____

_____

_____

_____

_____

_____

_____

4. Reread your poem. How does rereading it make you feel?

_____

_____

_____

_____

_____

_____

_____

_____

5. What meaning is there in this poem for you?

_____

_____

_____

_____

_____

_____

_____

_____

6. How were you able to make meaning from an otherwise random and meaningless series of words?

_____

_____

_____

_____

_____

_____

_____

7. Would you like to revise your poem? If so, why? If not, why not?

_____

_____

_____

_____

_____

_____

_____

_____

_____

_____

_____

_____

_____

PROCESS POINTS

- What does the poem tell you about yourself?
- Was this poem a journey of self-expression or self-discovery?
- Is poetry a form of self-expression you might use again. Why?

The Running Commentary

Overview

The running commentary, also sometimes known as the *bulletin board,* is designed to encourage the development of an ongoing internal dialogue throughout the day.

Instructions

This exercise will take place over the course of one day, or approximately 8 to 12 hours.

Purchase a small notebook that you can easily keep with you during the day, and write a question or thought on the first page.

Take out your notebook and reread your question or thought at least 5 times during the day, or whenever the original or related question or thought comes into your mind. Each time you reread the original question or thought, do one or more of the following:

- Write an answer to your original question or a reply to your thought
- Write your additional thoughts on the subject
- Write a new, but related, question
- Write an answer, reply, or response to any new questions or thoughts you may have jotted down as the day progresses

At the end of the day, review your original question or thought and all of your subsequent work in your notebook. Spend 5 to 10 minutes summarizing the work you completed for the day in this permanent journal.

THE EXERCISE

DAY: _____   DATE: _____

1. My original question or thought:

_____

_____

_____

_____

2.   Summary of how my day's running commentary developed:

_____

_____

_____

_____

_____

_____

_____

_____

_____

_____

_____

_____

_____

_____

_____

_____

_____

_____

_____

_____

_____

_____

3. How have I expanded on, or learned about, my original question?

_____

_____

_____

_____

_____

_____

_____

_____

_____

_____

_____

_____

_____

_____

_____

_____

_____

_____

PROCESS POINTS

- Did the running commentary help you to stay in touch with the same ideas, thoughts, feelings, or themes throughout the day?

- What have you learned about yourself from this exercise, or from the subject you spent the day discussing with yourself?

SECTION I

Review

- Having completed Section I, what have you learned about yourself and the process of journaling?

- Did you write in your journal every day, once each week, or in fits and starts? What did you learn about yourself and about the process of journaling?

- How much did you invest in the process of journaling, and what did you gain from it?

- Did you keep the promises you made at the beginning of this section? If not, why not?

- Are you prepared to renew your commitment to journaling before moving on to Section II?

SECTION II

Looking
in the Mirror

Who Are You?
Your Subpersonalities

Overview

You can use your journal to reflect different aspects of yourself. Many of us have experienced different feelings about the same event. For instance, you may be glad something happened and yet sorry at the same time. You may feel as though you should behave and react as an adult, and yet have a childlike side that feels different. You may have all sorts of conflicting feelings that you might normally try to *suppress* (purposely keep stuffed inside, away from anyone's sight—even your own) or difficult thoughts or memories you try to *repress* (unconsciously hide from yourself). Keeping a journal allows you to express these different feelings and different sides of you—those parts that you might otherwise keep hidden, even from yourself, because they are too difficult to be acknowledged. You can think of these inner parts as your subpersonalities.

Instructions

In exploring your subpersonalities, you will write from those points of view that represent how you may really feel about something, bringing to light a side of yourself that you may normally keep hidden. You can think of yourself as a system of feelings and thoughts that gets acted out by a set of behavior patterns. As people grow up, they develop a pattern of feelings, thoughts, and behaviors that they come to experience as *I*. In this case, *I = Self.*

But there is more to our selves than the *obvious* feelings, thoughts, and behaviors. In writing in your journal, aim to express and understand different aspects of your self and your subpersonalities, including:

- The childlike part of yourself
- The angry part of yourself
- The ashamed part of yourself
- The enraged part of yourself
- The weak part of yourself
- The proud part of yourself
- The shy part of yourself
- The generous part of yourself
- The selfish part of yourself

In the exercise, name and briefly describe as many parts of yourself as you can, and the conditions or circumstances under which you most feel these aspects of yourself emerging or coming close to the surface. Indicate how comfortable you are with these parts of yourself by writing a number from 1 to 5, where *1* equals "very *un*comfortable" and *5* equals "very comfortable."

Example

Name of this part of me	When do I most feel this part of me	1–5
Teacher: showing others what to do	When things are going wrong around me	4
Inner critic: doubting myself	In almost all new situations	1

THE EXERCISE

How many parts of yourself can you name? Some of these parts may be frightening or scary to you, or may even anger or disgust you because they're weak or sad or childlike. But remember, this is an opportunity to get to know your*self* in private, so don't be afraid to explore your own personality.

There are three steps to this process.

a. First name a part of your subpersonality and briefly describe what that part does.

b. Then describe the conditions under which that part is most likely to emerge or come close to the surface.

c. Finally, write a number from 1 to 5 that describes your level of comfort with that part of you, where:

> 1 = very *un*comfortable
> 2 = somewhat *un*comfortable
> 3 = neither *un*comfortable nor comfortable
> 4 = somewhat comfortable, and
> 5 = comfortable

	Name of this part of me	**When do I most feel this part of me**	**1–5**
1.	_____	_____	_____
2.	_____	_____	_____
3.	_____	_____	_____
4.	_____	_____	_____
5.	_____	_____	_____
6.	_____	_____	_____

Name of this part of me	When do I most feel this part of me	1–5
7. _____	_____	___
8. _____	_____	___
9. _____	_____	___
10. _____	_____	___
11. _____	_____	___
12. _____	_____	___
13. _____	_____	___
14. _____	_____	___
15. _____	_____	___
16. _____	_____	___
17. _____	_____	___
18. _____	_____	___
19. _____	_____	___
20. _____	_____	___

PROCESS POINTS

- Were you able to name different aspects of your personality? Was this difficult for you?

- Did you learn anything new about yourself?

- Does the idea that you have subpersonalities make you uncomfortable or does it free you up to explore yourself more deeply? Either way, what does this say about you?

Creating a Character Sketch

Overview

A character sketch is a written description of another person or a part of yourself. It's a good way to get to know someone, including yourself.

You can write a character sketch of:

- People you like or dislike

- Friends or family members

- Yourself, from the point of view of another person

- One of your subpersonalities: your inner child, your natural wisdom, your raging anger, your perfectionism, your internal critic, your inside healer, and so forth.

Instructions

For this exercise focus on creating a character sketch about yourself and, more specifically, one of your subpersonalities.

1. Close your eyes and imagine a particular part of yourself. What do you notice first? Feelings? The way this part of you looks?

2. Tune in to this part of you—what does this part of you like and dislike? What things and values are important to this part? What does this part need or want? What does this part fear? What do you and this part of you agree and disagree on? What upsets you about this part? What do you like about this part of you? What is the purpose of this part's life, and what is this part's role in your life? What would this part of you say if it could make a statement about the world and its role in it?

3. What are the qualities and attributes of this part: the good and the bad?

Don't worry. There isn't a right or wrong way to write a character sketch. You may decide that you love this part of you, need this part of you, or hate and fear this part of you. Again, there isn't a right or a wrong way—there's only an *honest* way.

THE EXERCISE

DAY: _____   DATE: _____

1. Does this part of you have a name? _____

2. What are the qualities and attributes of this part?

Good Qualities	*Bad Qualities*
_____	_____
_____	_____
_____	_____
_____	_____
_____	_____
_____	_____

3. What are the likes and dislikes of this part of you?

Likes	*Dislikes*
_____	_____
_____	_____
_____	_____
_____	_____
_____	_____

4. What things and values are important to this part of you?

_____

_____

_____

_____

_____

5.   What does this part of you need or want?

_____

_____

_____

_____

_____

6.   What does this part of you fear?

_____

_____

_____

_____

_____

7.   What do you and this part of you agree and disagree on?

Agree	*Disagree*
_____	_____
_____	_____
_____	_____
_____	_____
_____	_____

8.   What upsets you about this part of you?

_____

_____

_____

_____

_____

9. What do you like and dislike about this part of you?

Like   *Dislike*

_____   _____

_____   _____

_____   _____

_____   _____

_____   _____

_____   _____

10. What is the purpose of this part's life, and what is this part's role in your life?

_____

_____

_____

_____

_____

_____

_____

11. What would this part of you say if it could make a statement about the world and its role in it?

_____

_____

_____

_____

_____

_____

_____

12. Write a brief, general character sketch about this part of you.

_____

_____

_____

_____

_____

_____

_____

_____

_____

_____

_____

_____

_____

_____

_____

_____

_____

_____

PROCESS POINTS

- Was it difficult or uncomfortable describing yourself from a perspective different from the one you would normally take? Why?

- Did you learn anything about yourself by creating a sketch of only one part of yourself? If so, what did you learn? Were you unsettled or gratified by what you learned?

- Did this exercise leave you feeling that there are many facets of your personality yet to address or explore? If you didn't learn anything about yourself, why not?

How Do You
See Things from Within?

Overview

If you've completed Exercise 12, you've written a character sketch of at least one specific aspect of yourself—one of your subpersonalities. By now, you've become a little more familiar with one or more of your subparts. Now explore how that part of you sees the world.

Instructions

Pick a situation that you'd like to explore from the perspective of one or more of your subpersonalities. The situation can be anything you'd like to investigate further: a pleasant or unpleasant situation, a fun event, or a sad event.

THE EXERCISE

DAY: _____   DATE: _____

1. Describe a situation or event on which you'd like to reflect:

    _____

    _____

    _____

    _____

    _____

2. List those parts of yourself that you'd like to use to explore this situation:

    _____   _____

    _____   _____

    _____   _____

    _____   _____

3. Select one of these parts. Try to assume the point of view of this part of you. How does your subpersonality feel about the situation you described above? Let your feelings and thoughts fly. Don't hold back.

_____

_____

_____

_____

_____

_____

_____

_____

_____

_____

_____

_____

_____

_____

_____

_____

_____

_____

PROCESS POINTS

- What prompted your choice of situations to reflect upon? Were you being really honest with yourself in describing how you feel (or how part of you feels) about that situation? If not, what held you back from describing your real feelings?

- Were you able to get inside of yourself and explore your feelings from another perspective? Have you been selecting only those parts of your personality that you're comfortable with, or have you been pushing yourself to go further?

- Is it uncomfortable being pushed to explore aspects of your personality that you normally choose to overlook or suppress, or don't even want to acknowledge?

The Dialogue:
Talking to Yourself

Overview

A "dialogue" is nothing more than a conversation between two or more people. Because you have subparts to your personality, you can also have a dialogue with yourself. In this exercise, you'll let different aspects of yourself converse.

Instructions

Decide which of your subparts you would like to dialogue with each other. Who do you want in on this written conversation between you and yourself? You might have your angry side talk to your soothing side. Or maybe your inner child wants to dialogue with your controlling parent. Once you pick the parts, script the conversation you'd imagine them having. For example, a written dialogue between your compassionate self and a part of you named *rage* may develop like this:

compassionate self: Can you tell me why you get in the way of all my relationships?

rage: They have all let me down in the past. They have no value. And you are a sorry specimen for even needing anyone else. Maybe if you'd explain, I could alleviate your pain.

compassionate self: Your fury just ruins my life. I don't understand it, where it comes from.

rage: If you got rid of my pain, then where would you be? I protect you.

THE EXERCISE

How do you start? Just take the plunge, and begin.

DAY: _____   DATE: _____

Part A: _____   Statement 1: _____

_____

_____

_____

Part B: _____   Response 1: _____

_____

_____

_____

Part A: _____   Statement 2: _____

_____

_____

_____

Part B: _____   Response 2: _____

_____

_____

_____

Part A: _____   Statement 3: _____

_____

_____

_____

Part B: _____   Response 3: _____

_____

_____

_____

Part A: _____   Statement 4: _____

_____

_____

_____

Part B: _____   Response 4: _____

_____

_____

_____

Part A: _____   Statement 5: _____

_____

_____

_____

Part B: _____   Response 5: _____

_____

_____

_____

Part A: _____   Statement 6: _____

_____

_____

_____

Part B: _____   Response 6: _____

_____

_____

_____

Part A: _____   Statement 7: _____

_____

_____

_____

Part B: _____   Response 7: _____

_____

_____

_____

Part A: _____   Statement 8: _____

_____

_____

_____

Part B: _____   Response 8: _____

_____

_____

_____

Part A: _____   Statement 9: _____

_____

_____

_____

Part B: _____   Response 9: _____

_____

_____

_____

Part A: _____   Statement 10: _____

_____

_____

_____

Part B: _____   Response 10: _____

_____

_____

_____

Part A: _____   Statement 11: _____

_____

_____

_____

Part B: _____   Response 11: _____

_____

_____

_____

Part A: _____ Statement 12: _____

_____

_____

_____

Part B: _____ Response 12: _____

_____

_____

_____

Part A: _____ Statement 13: _____

_____

_____

_____

Part B: _____ Response 13: _____

_____

_____

_____

PROCESS POINTS

- What prompted your choice of subpersonalities for this exercise?

- How strange was it for you to have this dialogue? Did you feel that you were genuinely talking to yourself, or was it simply an exercise in creative writing for you?

- Did the conversation flow more easily than you thought it might? Did the exercise take over at some point?

EXERCISE 15

The Inner Map

Overview

We've been exploring the idea that people have subpersonalities and inner worlds. In this exercise we want to help you create a map of that inner world.

The Map

As you develop a sense of your subpersonalities—those aspects of yourself that lie hidden beneath the surface, perhaps even on a preconscious level—you are in a position to create a map of your central personality and its parts. The purpose of this map is the same as that for any map—to give you a picture of the territory and help you navigate your way. The map can be drawn in any number of ways.

- *You can draw the map to look like the floor plan of a house.* Where do you (your central personality—the you known to the world) live in the house? Which room do you occupy? In which rooms do other aspects of you live? Are they in the same room, the next room, or on the same floor? Who lives in big rooms and who lives in smaller rooms? Where you locate these different subpersonalities suggests the importance and power (influence) they have over your feelings and decisions, and how close they may be to one another and the surface.

- *Or you can draw the map to look like a suburban block.* Where do you live on the block? Where do other parts live? Which parts live near you and which live around the corner? Which parts are the closest to you and which parts are closest to one another?

The point is to become increasingly aware of how you function, your complexity, and the importance of self-knowledge. You'll also get a sense of how close you are to knowing these other aspects of yourself, and their distance from your consciousness.

Instructions

1. Although there are many ways to draw this map, in this exercise you'll draw your map to look like a solar system. Each subpersonality is drawn like a circle. Start with yourself in the center of the page, and then begin to add other circles with the name of that part of you written inside each of them. The parts that you feel the closest to, you can draw close by you. The parts you feel the most distant from, draw further away. Parts that are clear and dominant should be drawn large. Parts that are vague and less defined should be drawn small.

2. We use the term *syntonic* to describe ideas and feelings that we like, and the term *dystonic* to describe ideas and feelings that we don't like. Use connecting lines from each part to the central you to demonstrate whether the feelings and thoughts of that part are syntonic, dystonic, or unclear.

- ——— Use a solid line to show that the connection is syntonic.

- ═══ Use a double solid line to show an especially strong connection.

- VVVV Use a jagged line to show that the ideas and feelings associated with that part are dystonic and uncomfortable.

- WWW Use a double jagged line in cases where the connection is especially uncomfortable and dystonic.

- ·········· Use a dotted line to show indifference—that is, the relationship is neither syntonic nor dystonic.

- - - - - Use a dashed line to show vagueness or uncertainty about the connection.

- Where you really are uncertain about the type of connection, draw either a straight, jagged, or dashed line, with one or two strike marks through it to demonstrate your uncertainty.

- Use other symbols, or colored pens or pencils if you like. The object is to map your inner world so that you can see it on paper.

Changing the Map

As you get to know yourself and become more aware of your subpersonalities, your map is likely to change. As a reflection of you, it's dynamic and changes over time—it's not a static map that never changes. It may change as some aspects of yourself become more dominate over time and others grow more distant. Some connections that feel dystonic now may become syntonic later. You may become aware of new aspects of yourself. Revisit your map every so often.

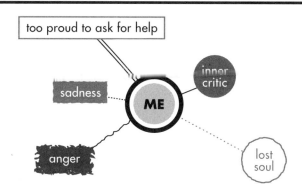

THE EXERCISE

Remember, this map is *dynamic*. That is, today is just a starting point as you get to know yourself and map your inside world. It is dynamic because it may change and grow because you are changing and growing.

DAY: _____   DATE: _____

PROCESS POINTS

- Did the map help you learn more about yourself and your subpersonalities? What did you learn about yourself?

- How did this exercise leave you feeling?

- Are you likely to continue developing and exploring your map?

My Feelings

Overview

Feelings are funny things. Not everybody can recognize them in themselves at any given time. This exercise is designed to help you to recognize feelings in yourself. It will also aid you in understanding *why* you may be feeling a certain way at that particular moment.

Instructions

Use this worksheet to help identify your feelings and thoughts at any time, such as during groups, at a meeting, reading a book, thinking quietly. It can be an aid to making sense of what's going on inside of you, and why.

THE EXERCISE

My Feelings

DAY: _____ DATE: _____

How am I feeling?   *Why am I feeling this way?*

_____ Agitated   _____

_____ Amused   _____

_____ Annoyed   _____

_____ Angry   _____

_____ Anxious   _____

_____ Betrayed   _____

_____ Concerned   _____

_____ Confused   _____

_____ Foolish   _____

_____ Frustrated   _____

_____ Happy   _____

How am I feeling?   *Why am I feeling this way?*

_____ Hopeful   _____

_____ Hopeless   _____

_____ Ignored   _____

_____ Incapable   _____

_____ Incompetent   _____

_____ Irritated   _____

_____ Joyful   _____

_____ Let down   _____

_____ Sad   _____

_____ Scared   _____

_____ Trapped   _____

_____ Unhappy   _____

_____ Worried   _____

_____ Worthless   _____

_____   _____

_____   _____

_____   _____

_____   _____

PROCESS POINTS

- Was it easy for you to recognize your feelings? Do you normally know how you're feeling at any given moment?

- Was it easy for you to understand why you were having those feelings? Do you normally know what evokes your feelings at any given moment?

- Did the exercise help you to better understand your feelings and what evokes them?

EXERCISE ⟨17⟩

Dreams and
Their Meanings

Overview

No one really understands why people dream. However, most people believe that dreams have a specific purpose of some kind, and many believe that dreams have meaning. Your dreams and how you view them tell you something about your thoughts, your desires, your feelings, and your fears.

Those who believe in the analysis of dreams, believe that dreams have *projective* meaning; that is, dreams project into our conscious mind some experience from our unconscious mind. Through the interpretation of dreams, then, it may be possible to understand something more about yourself.

Many people who want to remember, study, and make sense out of their dreams keep a dream journal—a log of what happened in their dreams, and their possible meanings. When logging a dream, record both the *manifest* content and the *latent* content. Manifest content comprises images that are simply the reflections of thoughts, ideas, and experiences often already in short-term memory from the day or evening immediately before a dream. That is, you may dream about a yellow school bus because you passed one on the way home from work and noticed it had broken down. That image remained in your memory.

The latent content of dreams comprises the feelings, ideas, and thoughts under-lying the manifest images. The latent content is the *hidden* content of dreams. You may have dreamed about a yellow school bus, but in your dream you experienced the bus as soothing and safe. The *image* of a school bus taken from your actual waking experiences during the dream day (the day and evening prior to the dream) is a sub-stitute for and represents a *feeling* of safety and security, perhaps because when you were a child, going to school was a nurturing experience. Some part of this dream, then, is about safety and not about school buses. The school bus is simply a conve-nient graphic image that can represent a feeling that is not otherwise easily depicted in a dream, because feelings themselves are not visible.

Some people dream of getting lost on some form of transportation, where the *manifest* image of getting lost on a bus or train is actually a stand-in for *latent* anx-iety about getting lost or sidetracked in their life. People dream about going out naked, where the manifest content is about being unclothed in public and the latent content may be about anxiety, humiliation, and loss of control. This exercise focuses on discovering why the latent issue is on your mind and on helping you explore your life and search beneath the obvious.

Instructions

The instructions for completing the exercise are self-explanatory and are provided
on the worksheet, step-by-step.

THE EXERCISE

DAY: _____   DATE: _____

1. Begin the exercise by writing down the details of a dream you recently had, or a dream that
    has stuck in your mind. Provide a written sketch or a more detailed description, if you like.

    _____

    _____

    _____

    _____

    _____

    _____

    _____

2. What were the most powerful images in the dream? Following is a checklist of different
    images to help free up your memories of the dream. Use the checklist to help focus on
    which images were the clearest or had the strongest "feel" to them in your dream.

    ___ location of the dream   ___ familiar location   ___ unfamiliar location

    ___ crowds of people   ___ absence of people   ___ a specific person

    ___ strangers in the dream   ___ injury to self   ___ injury to other

    ___ accidents/disasters   ___ animals or insects   ___ transportation

    ___ colors   ___ unusual events   ___ buildings

    ___ words that were spoken   ___ silence   ___ clocks

    Other dream images you most easily recall:

    _____   _____

    _____   _____

    _____   _____

    _____   _____

3. Did you see any of the dream images or have any of the dream experiences in your waking or real life during the evening or day immediately before the dream?

_____

_____

_____

_____

_____

_____

_____

_____

4. Why do you think these images appeared in your dream? What was their significance?

_____

_____

_____

_____

_____

_____

_____

5. How important were these images to the meaning or feel of the dream?

_____

_____

_____

_____

_____

_____

_____

6. What were your most powerful feelings in the dream? Following is a checklist of different feelings to help free up your memories of the dream. Use the checklist to help focus on those feelings that were the most powerful in your dream.

___ sadness	___ happiness	___ fun
___ fear	___ confusion	___ loss
___ anger	___ anxiety	___ panic
___ satisfaction	___ frustration	___ pity
___ grief	___ amusement	___ betrayal
___ hopeless	___ hopeful	___ trapped

Other dream feelings you most easily recall:

_____   _____

_____   _____

_____   _____

7. How were the *feelings* in your dream related to the *images* in the dream?

_____

_____

_____

_____

_____

_____

_____

8. Is there some issue in your life right now that may have been the "seed" for your dream? Can you relate the feelings in your dream to what's happening in your life?

_____

_____

_____

_____

_____

_____

9. How does this dream reflect some part of your life or the way you see or approach life?

_____

_____

_____

_____

_____

_____

_____

10. What does this dream tell you about yourself or an issue in your life? What is the meaning of the dream?

_____

_____

_____

_____

_____

_____

_____

_____

PROCESS POINTS

- Did the exercise provide you with a different way of understanding your dreams?

- How do you feel now? Was the process of dream interpretation useful, interesting, or emotionally difficult? What have you learned?

- Can you pick out repeating themes in your dreams? Do these themes have meaning—are they messages or just meaningless symbols?

Review

- Now that you've completed Section II, have you discovered things about yourself you did not know before?

- About which newly discovered parts of yourself will it be helpful to know more? How will this knowledge help you?

- Which parts of yourself would you like to know about? Which aspects of yourself are the most troubling to you? Would you like to spend more time learning about a particular aspect of yourself before moving onto Section III?

- Did you keep your commitments to openness and honesty as you worked in Section II? Are you ready to renew your commitments before moving on to Section III?

SECTION III

Seeing Yourself in the World

Process Recording

Overview

This exercise can help you to look at any situation from a variety of perspectives and gives you the opportunity to pull your thoughts together as you make sense of the situation. As you work through this exercise, you move from the most objective perspective to the most subjective as you physically move across the page.

The first perspective is called *content*—what actually happened from the most objective and emotionless perspective possible. Content simply reflects a sequence of events in much the same way as a movie camera recording a scene captures the facts, and just the facts.

Process refers to the way things happened—not just the objective facts but the "how" of what happened. Process tends to be less *objective* (the facts) and more *subjective* (the underlying tone). You can also look at an event from a *feeling* perspective, logging the emotions that are evoked for you as you watch or are involved in the situation.

The fourth perspective—*analysis and review*—provides a look backwards, an attempt to make sense out of what happened and its effects on the people involved, including, most of all, you.

Instructions

Pick an event of significance in your life.

1. Use the left-hand column (*content*) to objectively log what happened:

   - Be a movie camera. What happened and in what order?
   - Describe the objective facts. What would an observer have seen in the interaction?
   - Attempt no interpretation. Don't try to figure out what the interaction actually was about.

2. In the center column (*process*) add your reflections on underlying issues and dynamics:

   - Replay the contents to discover otherwise hidden levels of the interaction—those which an observer would not easily see.
   - Try to make sense of how and why things happened.
   - Describe the hidden, underlying tone of the interaction.
   - Illuminate and make visible what was happening beneath the surface.

3. In the right-hand column (*feelings/evaluation*) add words or short sentences that describe how you felt about the situation as it unfolded:

   • Go a little deeper. Capture feelings, meaning, and the forces at work.

   • Describe how you were feeling at that moment.

   • Try to remember what was motivating you at that moment.

   • What shaped the interaction as it developed?

4. In the lower section (*analysis and review*) reflect on and assess the material you described in the three sections above. Here you can look at the event and its impact on you:

   • What happened and why?

   • How did you feel before, during, and after the interaction?

   • Did your feelings change during the interaction, and why?

   • What could you have done differently?

   • What was your role in making things better or worse?

   • What have you learned about yourself?

   • What have you learned about others?

   • What have you learned about the way you interact with others?

Example

PROCESS RECORDING FOR EVENT: <u>FIGHT WITH SALLY</u>

Content	Process	Feelings/Evaluation
1. When Sally told me she forgot to return my books, I started arguing with her.	We often argue about small issues. This argument fell into the usual pattern.	I became immediately annoyed.
2. Sally told me I'm always picking arguments with her for no good reason.	Sally falls into an old pattern of almost at once attacking my motives.	I feel frustrated. We can't discuss issues.
3. I told Sally that she's always doing things that lead to arguments and that I think she purposely does them.	I put the blame back on Sally.	I go on the attack.

(Continued)

4. Sally said she's leaving. I said that if she does, she shouldn't expect me to loan her anything again.	Sally becomes infuriated with me, threatening to leave. I up the stakes by trying to force her to stay.	I feel frustrated because I can't make my point if Sally leaves. I don't want her to go.
5. Sally angrily said she's always lending me things that I don't return on time or that I return damaged.	Sally stays but launches into a counterattack on my faults, turning the issue around. Voices are louder.	Now I feel defensive because I'm being attacked. I try to regain the upper hand.
6. I angrily deny this and say that I won't borrow anything from her again.	I stop Sally's attack on me through denial and refusal to borrow from her again. I'm still upping the stakes.	I try to stop her attack and attempt to get back on top.
7. Sally says that's fine and heads for the door.	Sally is at a loss for words.	We both feel frustrated now.
8. I yell at Sally to come back, but she continues to head for the door.	I try to stop her by intimidation.	I feel angry. I don't want her to cop out.
9. I say that if she goes, I won't be here later.	Frustrated, I threaten Sally, again upping the stakes.	I feel powerless. I launch into another attack.

ANALYSIS AND REVIEW

I feel the same old frustration with the same old patterns. I was angry with Sally before she even came into the room. My anger had less to do with her borrowing the books than with her apparent lack of respect for me or my property. But by immediately attacking Sally, I sent her right into a defensive mode where she protected herself by not listening to what I was actually saying and by attacking me right back. So, right away, I got into a no-win situation. By pushing Sally, I forced her to either roll over or push back, and I couldn't have been satisfied in either case. We wound up both trying to win, instead of both trying to deal with the *real* issues of mutual respect, trust, and how frustrated we both feel in our relationship.

THE EXERCISE

Process Recording for Event: _____

DAY: _____ DATE: _____

Content	Process	Feelings/Evaluation

ANALYSIS AND REVIEW

_____
_____
_____
_____
_____
_____
_____
_____
_____
_____
_____
_____
_____
_____
_____
_____
_____
_____
_____

PROCESS POINTS

- Was it difficult to view, and review, the same event from several different perspectives?

- Did process recording help you to understand an event from more than one perspective?

- Did process recording help you to better understand the difference between content and process? Has the process-recording method helped you to see events in your life a little differently?

Shifting Perspectives

Overview

In the movie *Rashomon,* the same situation is replayed for the audience from the viewpoint of four different people. Each point of view is correct from that person's perspective. The movie illustrates the idea that meaning in any interaction or event is not static and unchanging, but based on context and what the participant brings to the situation. In this exercise you'll learn to shift perspectives by describing a situation from not only your own point of view as a participant, but also from the perspective of another participant in the same event, and from the perspective of a bystander—someone who was not involved but witnessed the event from the outside.

Instructions

1. Select a situation in your life in which there was some conflict between the way you saw things and the way things were seen or understood by another participant in the same event.

2. Describe the interaction from your perspective:
   - What happened?
   - Why did it happen?
   - How did it happen?
   - How did you feel about it as it was happening?
   - What was the outcome?

3. Now describe the same event from the perspective of at least one other person who was involved in that interaction. Put yourself in this person's shoes, and see the event through his or her eyes. Answer the same questions, but from this other person's point of view.

4. Finally, describe the same interaction but this time from the perspective of an outside observer, someone who was not involved in the interaction but who was a "fly on the wall." Answer the same questions, but from the point of view of this totally impartial observer.

THE EXERCISE

1. Pick an event and describe what happened in purely objective terms. That is, don't explain your feelings or thoughts on the subject—just present the facts of the situation.

_____

_____

_____

_____

_____

_____

_____

_____

_____

_____

2. Now describe the situation or interaction from your own perspective.

_____

_____

_____

_____

_____

_____

_____

_____

_____

_____

3.　Again describe the same situation, but from the subjective perspective of one of the other participants.

_____

_____

_____

_____

_____

_____

_____

4.　Describe the same event yet again, but this time from the perspective of an uninvolved third party who happened to observe the situation without being involved in it, and who has no deep feelings about it. How would this person explain what happened?

_____

_____

_____

_____

_____

_____

_____

PROCESS POINTS
- Is it possible to have different views about the same situation, each of which is "correct?"
- What have you learned about yourself and your behavior, and the points of view and behaviors of others?
- What have you learned about the way others might _legitimately_ see you, even though you may normally disagree with their points of view or their criticisms?

What If I Were Wrong . . .

Overview

This exercise builds on the idea that people are subjective beings. That is, people experience the world through a filter of emotions, beliefs, and ideas that may prevent them from seeing another point of view or hearing another opinion. This is particularly true of how people view their own behavior.

By asking the question "what if I were wrong," you'll get the chance to rethink the situation, your feelings about it, the conclusions you reached, and your behavior following the event. In short, you'll get the chance to think things through from another, more objective perspective.

Instructions

1. Pick an event in which there was some conflict with another person—a friend, a family member, a coworker, or a stranger in a store. This conflict must be one in which you are sure *you* were right and the other person was wrong.

   - Describe the event from your own point of view.
   - Describe how you behaved during the interaction.
   - Describe any opinion you may have held prior to the interaction about the other person.
   - Describe what motives you ascribed to the other person to explain her or his behavior.
   - Describe how you felt about the other person after the interaction ended.
   - Describe how you generally felt after the conflict ended.
   - Describe how you behaved toward the other person after the conflict ended or in general.

2. Now ask yourself this question: "What if I were wrong?"

   - Describe the event from the other person's point of view.
   - Describe how you might have behaved during the interaction if you believed *you* were wrong and *not* the other person.
   - Describe how any opinion you may have held prior to the interaction about the other person or the situation itself would have changed had you realized you were wrong in this situation.
   - Describe what you think the other person's motives *actually* were in the situation, assuming you were wrong about the person or the situation.

- Describe how you might have felt about the other person after the interaction ended had you believed you were wrong in this situation.
- Describe how you might have felt after the conflict ended, had you believed you were wrong.
- Describe how your behavior might have been different after the conflict ended, had you believed you were wrong.

3. Finally, ask yourself if it's possible that you *have* been wrong about the way things happened, the other person, or the other person's motives, but have not been able to see it.

THE EXERCISE

1. **Part One: I'm Right.**

   a. Describe a conflict with another person from your own point of view.

   _____

   _____

   _____

   _____

   _____

   b. How did you behave during the interaction?

   _____

   _____

   _____

   _____

   _____

   c. Did you hold any opinions about the other person or the situation even before this incident? What were they?

   _____

   _____

   _____

   _____

   _____

d. Why do you think the other person behaved as he or she did? What were his or her motives in this situation?

_____

_____

_____

_____

_____

e. How did you feel about the other person after the interaction ended? What was your opinion of the other person after the interaction ended?

_____

_____

_____

_____

_____

f. How did you feel, generally speaking, after the conflict was over?

_____

_____

_____

_____

_____

g. How did you behave after the conflict was over, either toward the other person or in general?

_____

_____

_____

_____

_____

h.   How do you know you were right?

_____

_____

_____

_____

_____

2.   Part Two: What If I Were Wrong?

a.   Describe the event from the other person's point of view.

_____

_____

_____

_____

_____

b.   How might your behavior have been different during the interaction, had you believed you were wrong in this situation?

_____

_____

_____

_____

_____

c.   Is it possible that any preformed opinions you held about the other person or the type of situation might have changed during the interaction had you believed you were wrong? How might these opinions have changed?

_____

_____

_____

_____

_____

d. If you believe you were wrong in this situation, how might you now understand the other person's motives in the situation?

_____

_____

_____

_____

_____

e. How might you have felt about the other person after the interaction ended, had you believed you were wrong in this situation?

_____

_____

_____

_____

_____

f. How might you have felt after the conflict ended, had you believed you were wrong in this situation?

_____

_____

_____

_____

_____

g. How might your behavior have been different after the conflict ended, had you believed you were wrong in this situation?

_____

_____

_____

_____

_____

h.   Is it possible that you *might have been wrong* about the way things happened in the situation you just described, about the other person, the other person's motives, and so on?

_____

_____

_____

_____

_____

_____

_____

_____

_____

_____

_____

PROCESS POINTS

- Has this exercise changed the way you see things at all? If your answer is yes, then what might stop you from seeing that things aren't always as you believe them to be? What does this say about you and about the way in which you see the world?

- What do you bring into situations that sometimes clouds your ability to see things from another perspective?

The Artist's Way

Overview

People often travel the same paths daily. You see the same sights and the same people and fall into the same routine. In doing so, it is easy to lose sight of those things that are outside of the daily routine. You may not notice the way that light changes in the sky at different times of the day and year. You may not notice that a coworker has changed the way he or she looks. You may not know the names of the side streets you travel along, or the exit number you take as you get off the highway each day on the way to work. You may be blind to the small things because they are overshadowed by the larger daily features of your life. You may not see the trees for the forest.

Conversely, it is the artist's way to not miss seeing things—to capture those tiny details that make up a personality, an experience, a transaction, and life as it passes along. In this exercise, you'll learn to look at your life through an artist's eyes.

Instructions

This exercise lasts for 1 week and should be completed in 7 consecutive days. You will pick one "thing" to notice for each day of the exercise, making seven things in all that you will seek out.

These things can be anything you want, but they must be things that you normally don't notice in your daily life. For example:

- The number of yellow doors you pass on the way to work
- The number of different trees you see during the day
- The type of socks your coworkers wear
- Your own attitude about the things you hear, see, or otherwise experience during the day
- The number of times during the day you hear an expression or jargon
- The way that light and shadows fall as the day passes
- The number of churches in your neighborhood and the number of different architectural church designs
- The number of times you get angry, frustrated, embarrassed, or experience a particular feeling
- The number of times you see the same advertisement or type of advertisement on TV

- The number of advertisements aimed at a particular audience that you see in magazines
- The type of camera angles and editing cuts used in different television shows

Once you notice something new, you'll describe how it feels to see it for the first time and what has stopped you, until now, from previously seeing what you are now consciously observing.

THE EXERCISE

Make seven copies for this exercise.

DAY: _____ DATE: _____ DAY #: _____

1. What item, interaction, or thing were you observing for this day?

_____

2. Why did you made this choice?

_____

_____

3. Describe your experience as you observed the item(s) you focused on for this day.

_____

_____

_____

_____

_____

4. Did you find the experience difficult? Did you forget to observe as the day moved on?

_____

_____

_____

_____

_____

5.   Did you learn anything about yourself from the experience?

_____

_____

_____

_____

_____

6.   Did you learn anything about anyone or anything else from the experience?

_____

_____

_____

_____

_____

7.   What did you learn?

_____

_____

_____

_____

_____

8.   What was it like to be an observer today?

_____

_____

_____

_____

_____

9.   Did being an observer got in the way of your normal day, or did it enhance your normal day?

_____

_____

_____

_____

10. If this is day 2 or beyond, is it getting easier to be an observer? Why?

_____

_____

_____

_____

_____

_____

11. What about you has changed as a result of being an observer?

_____

_____

_____

_____

_____

_____

12. Do you want to continue to be an observer, even once the exercise is over?

_____

_____

_____

_____

_____

_____

13. What will prevent you from being an observer once this exercise ends? What stops you under normal circumstances from "seeing?"

_____

_____

_____

_____

_____

_____

14. What is about *you*—your attitudes, your beliefs, your habits—that stops you from seeing more clearly more of the time?

_____

_____

_____

_____

_____

_____

_____

_____

_____

_____

_____

PROCESS POINTS

- Were you surprised by what you saw once you started to observe?
- Did you change much over the 7 days of the exercise? Did you recognize daily, incremental changes as you completed the exercise each day?
- In retrospect, have you changed at all as a result of the exercise?

Letters

Overview

Is there anyone, living or deceased, to whom you have some things to say that you have not fully said before? You might want to say something that is loving, angry, vengeful, sad, confrontational, embarrassing to you, or some combination of feelings. The sentiment isn't the issue. What matters is that you have something to state—or perhaps restate.

In this exercise, you will write that person a letter. In that letter, you will say all those things you want to say, any way you want to say them.

Instructions

1. The first draft of your letter will be a *keeper* letter. That is, you will not send the letter—you will *keep* it.

2. You may want to write the letter again in a second and more defined draft. This second draft may also be a keeper letter. You may even prepare a third draft. Keep rereading and revising until you are completely satisfied with the letter.

3. After you've reviewed your keeper letter and made changes to your satisfaction, you may decide that the letter will always be a keeper letter. Of course, you may also decide to mail it to the person for whom it was intended, if that person is still alive. In this case, your keeper letter turns into a *sender*.

THE EXERCISE

DAY: _____   DATE: _____

Write your letter. Write it any way you want. Once written, reread it, and decide if you need a rewrite or a second draft. You may want to show the letter to someone for feedback. Write the letter on a separate page, in case you decide to send it.

Letter to: Walter

DRAFT # 1.   DAY: 1/16/99   DATE: Saturday

Dear Walt,

Over the past 14 years I have thought colored
many times they were that you have worked so hard
to deal with your alcoholism, and

Letter to: _____

DRAFT # 2.   DAY: _____   DATE: _____

_____

_____

_____

_____

_____

_____

_____

_____

_____

_____

_____

_____

_____

_____

_____

_____

_____

_____

_____

_____

_____

_____

_____

_____

_____

_____

_____

_____

_____

PROCESS POINTS

- Did the final draft of your letter say what you wanted it to? If not, why not?

- Did the final draft relieve your feelings? If it did, why? If it didn't, why not?

- Will you keep the letter or will you send it? In either case, why?

- What has writing this letter taught you about yourself? What has your decision to either keep or send the letter taught you about yourself?

An Important Possession

Overview

People can, of course, have relationships with other people. They can also have relationships with things. Different objects are important to us at different stages in our lives. Young children want objects that comfort them. As they age, they want objects with which they can play, then tools they can use, and then things to remind them of accomplishments or significant aspects of their lives.

In this exercise, select an object that is important to you now and concentrate on how it looks, how it feels, how you would describe it, and the nature of its meaning to you.

Instructions

1. You must first decide which inanimate object in your life is most important to you. Imagine that you have to leave your home and may take only one object with you. Find that object and place it in front of you. Look at it carefully. Study its shape and its texture. Touch it and lift it if you can.

2. In the space provided, draw the object. Don't worry if you can't draw well, just do the best you can. You may want to make one drawing or a series of drawings from different angles or in different colors, mediums, or styles.

3. Below the drawing, describe the object as you would to someone with no sight, or by phone to someone who has never seen this object or any object like it before.

4. Then write about why the object is so important to you, what it means to you, what it says about who you are.

THE EXERCISE

1. The object most important to me is _____

2. Draw the object. Don't worry if you can't draw (or you feel you can't draw), just do the best you can. You may want to make one drawing or a series of drawings from different angles or in different colors, mediums, or styles.

3. Describe the object as you would to someone with no sight, or by phone to someone who has never seen this object or any object like it before.

_____

_____

_____

_____

_____

_____

_____

_____

_____

_____

4. Describe why this object is so important to you: Why did you select this object? What does it mean to you? What does it say about who you are?

_____

_____

_____

_____

_____

_____

_____

_____

_____

_____

_____

_____

_____

PROCESS POINTS

- Were you surprised at how much or how little you knew about an object that is so important to you?

- Did you learn anything about yourself by thinking about this object and its value to you?

- What object might you have selected for this exercise ten years ago, and why? What object do you think might be important to you ten years from now, and why?

- What do these changes say about you as you move through your life?

A List

Overview

Lists can be magical. There is something about them that helps us concentrate and makes us pay attention to them. There is something, perhaps, about the power of repetition. Lists have rhythm. Lists turn the written word into poetry.

Instructions

Pick a topic for your list. It can be anything about which you can make a list:

- What's on your mind today.
- Your favorite food.
- What you like about work.
- What you like about someone you love.
- What you dislike about someone you love.
- Places you have visited.
- Places you would like to visit.

Name the topic, and beneath it list as many things about your topic as you can, one item on each line below the topic.

Then review your list and write about what you've learned from it: about the topic itself and about yourself.

THE EXERCISE

DAY: _____   DATE: _____

The topic: _____

The list: _____

_____

_____

_____

_____

_____

_____

_____

_____

_____

_____

_____

_____

_____

Why did you pick this particular topic?

_____

_____

_____

_____

_____

_____

_____

PROCESS POINTS

- Did you learn anything about yourself by thinking about the topic and its meaning to you?

- What have you learned about the topic itself from your list?

- What have you learned about yourself from your list?

Review

- In Section I you focused on approaches to journaling, and in Section II on your relationship with yourself. In Section III, you examined your relationships with others and the external world. Was one of these sections more difficult for you than the others? Do you have more trouble understanding and managing yourself or others?

- Was it harder for you to be open and honest in Section II or Section III?

- Before moving on to Section IV, review and renew your commitments.

Recording
Your History

Daily Diary
of Thoughts and Feelings

Overview

You can use your journal as a diary or record of your daily life. You can use it to make your way through the day, noting important events and your emotional or intellectual response to them. You can use it as a tool to analyze what goes on in your head and heart as life happens around you, to you, and with you.

Instructions

Use this worksheet to help learn how to record, review, and contemplate your life. Focus on:

- What
- Where
- When
- Who
- How
- The meaning of events in and aspects of your daily life

THE EXERCISE

DAY: _____   DATE: _____

1. Describe a major event of your day, something you would like to remember—a situation, interaction, or observation that had some impact on you today.

    _____

    _____

    _____

    _____

    _____

2.   Why is it important to remember this event? Describe the impact of the event on you.

_____

_____

_____

_____

_____

_____

_____

_____

3.   Why did this particular event have meaning for you?

_____

_____

_____

_____

_____

_____

_____

_____

4.   How did you _behave_ during or after the event?

_____

_____

_____

_____

_____

_____

_____

_____

5. How did you *feel* during and after the event?

_____

_____

_____

_____

_____

_____

_____

_____

6. Did the event teach you anything?

_____

_____

_____

_____

_____

_____

_____

7. Did the event remind you of other events in your life? In what way? How did the previous event affect your reaction to the event you described today?

_____

_____

_____

_____

_____

_____

_____

_____

PROCESS POINTS

- Did keeping a daily diary help you take a different view of your life and the events in and around it?

- What have you learned? About other people? About yourself? About your environment?

Life Markers: Events

Overview

How is your life today linked to your life in the past? How much has your past shaped your present? What were the important events in your life that served as the milestones leading from one phase of your personal development to the next?

Life markers is an exercise to help you reflect on the past, with special reference to how your present life has leapfrogged from one milestone, or life marker, to another.

Instructions

Life marker events

1. Pick six events in your life that you remember well. You don't have to recall all of the details exactly, just simple events that stand out in your mind. The events can be happy, sad, or just stand out for no reason you can think of. The day you . . .

   - Began elementary school
   - Moved to a new home
   - Got a pet
   - Lost a friend
   - Had your seventh birthday

2. Pick one of the events, write it down anywhere on a page, and circle it.

   - Now find a word or short phrase that summarizes the event and write it down next to the event, in quotation marks.
   - Below the event, write down feelings that you associate with that event or that day: sad, happy, mad, worried.
   - Next to the feelings write down one short phrase that describes why that day or that event was important to you: "the day I learned about being part of a family," "the day I learned about being alone," "the first time I felt awkward," or "the first time I felt powerful."
   - Draw a box around that phrase, or circle it in a different color.

3. Repeat the process for the second life-marking event that you've chosen. Continue until you've written about all six of the milestones you've selected. It doesn't matter where you place each life marker on the page, as long as you have room for each and you write clearly enough so that you can see what you've written.

4. Connect the life markers in chronological order, with a connecting line and arrow to indicate the sequence. Now you have a chronological map of some important markers in your life: days or events that influenced you in some way.

5. Look at the series of life markers you've selected. How are they connected? Next to the line that connects any two milestones, briefly list the features that the two events have in common.

Example

The example we've included only lists three life markers, but it will give you a sense of how to write down each marker.

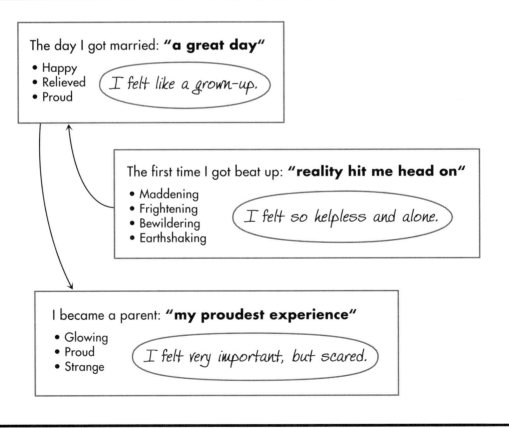

THE EXERCISE

Pick six points in your life that you remember well:

1. _____

2. _____

3. _____

4. _____

5. _____

6. _____

Now draw your events map, referring to steps 2 through 5 in the preceding list.

PROCESS POINTS

- How did the earlier life markers shape or influence the later markers? Would a later life event or marker have happened without the earlier marker first occurring? Is one particular marker important *because* of an earlier life marker?

- Is there a pattern to the life markers you've chosen? Are the markers you've picked widely divergent, or can you pick out a pattern of disappointment, empowerment, loss, success, or luck that somehow ties the different life markers together? Seek the pattern.

- What have you learned about yourself from looking at this web of life markers and its patterns? How has your life been shaped by these events, and how have these events worked together to form the person you are today?

EXERCISE 27
Life Markers: People

Overview

In Exercise 26 you looked at *events* in your life as life markers. In this exercise, you'll look at *people* who have served as significant markers in your life. These can include parents, teachers, friends, and others who have been important in your development.

Instructions

1. Pick six people in your life who had some meaningful effect on you, who stand out in your memory for one reason or another. Your memory of them can be good, bad, sad, fulfilling, or unfulfilling. People stand out in our memories for all sorts of reason. People who:

   - Helped you
   - Hurt you
   - Meant a lot to you
   - Annoyed you

2. Pick one of the people, and circle the name.

   - Next to the name write a word or short phrase in quotation marks that describes or characterizes that person.
   - Below the person's name write down feelings that you associate with that person: sad, happy, angry, scared, safe, etc.
   - Next to the name write down one short phrase that describes why that person was important to you: "the first bully I ever met," "my first love," "as my mother, she protected and supported me," "as my mother, she failed to protect and support me."

3. Repeat the process for the second significant person that you've chosen, and again until you've written about the six people you've selected. It doesn't matter where you place each person marker on the page, as long as you have room for each and you write clearly enough so that you can see what you've written.

4. Connect these significant people in chronological order, with a connecting line and arrow that indicates who came first in time. Now you have a chronological map of some of your life markers: people who have influenced you in some way.

5. Look at the series of people you've selected. How are they connected? Next to the line that connects any two milestones, briefly list the features that the two people have in common.

Example

Please refer to the example in Exercise 26 (Life Markers: Events). The format will be the same for this exercise.

THE EXERCISE

Pick six people in your life that you remember well:

1. _____

2. _____

3. _____

4. _____

5. _____

6. _____

Now draw your people map, referring to steps 2 through 8 in the preceding list.

PROCESS POINTS

- How did the earlier significant relationships shape or influence the later ones? Is there a pattern to the relationships you've chosen to describe? Would a later relationship have happened without the earlier relationship occurring? Would you have had the sort of emotional reaction to a particular person had it not been for an earlier relationship or experience? Is one particular relationship important *because* of an earlier life marker?

- Is there a pattern to the relationships you've chosen? Are the people you've picked different from one another or are there similarities. In these relationships, can you pick out a pattern of friendship, animosity, disappointment, love, or abuse that somehow ties the different relationships together.

- Reflect on what you've learned about yourself from looking at your web of significant relationships and its patterns, about how your life has been shaped by these relationships, and about how these relationships have come to form the person you are today.

EXERCISE  28

The Ten-Minute Autobiography

Overview

How you see yourself varies with your mood, the season, the people you are with at the time, recent events in your life, etc. Sometimes you feel good about yourself, sometimes not so good.

This exercise requires you to write an autobiographical sketch of your life in 10 minutes. By writing an autobiography in only 10 minutes, you focus on how you view yourself during those moments in time.

Instructions

Time yourself for this exercise. Ten minutes only! No cheating. If you like the idea of an autobiography, and want to take more time, do that later. Right now, concentrate on the goal of a 10-minute autobiography.

You can describe your life in any way you want. You can focus on your whole life, an interval in it, or even a single incident. You can shape your autobiography on a theme (for instance, strong influences on my life, memories I have never forgotten, my family), or you can try a free-flowing autobiography (see Exercise 8, Stream of Consciousness).

THE EXERCISE

DAY: _____   DATE: _____

Allow yourself 5 minutes to decide what you want to write about, and how. Time yourself.

1. Now take 10 minutes. No more and no less. Write your autobiography.

_____

_____

_____

_____

_____

_____

2. What does your autobiography reflect about today—the moment and circumstances surrounding you as you wrote it? Was the style, subject matter, or theme influenced by today in some way?

_____

_____

_____

_____

_____

_____

_____

_____

_____

3. If you had to write another autobiography, would you focus on the same subject matter and simply write it from another perspective, or would you choose another slice of or look at your life?

_____

_____

_____

_____

_____

_____

_____

_____

_____

PROCESS POINTS

- Look back at your autobiography. What does it say about you as a person? Does it offer an optimistic, upbeat view of who you are? Does it reflect a sense of high self-esteem, low self-esteem, indifference, or detachment?

- Did you discover anything important about yourself? Does your autobiography somehow reflect how you feel about yourself in general?

- Was the mood reflected in the autobiography determined or shaped by events in your present life?

EXERCISE  29

Another Ten-Minute Autobiography

Overview

In Exercise 28, The Ten-Minute Autobiography, you wrote a 10-minute auto-biography. Now look at yourself and your history, through a different lens. Pick a different day and write another 10-minute autobiography. Same rules, but this autobiography must include *none* of the material described in your first auto-biography.

Instructions

We *don't* want you to write this second autobiography on the same day as your first. Once again, time yourself for this exercise, allowing 10 minutes only.

Again, you can describe your life in any way you want. You can describe your whole life, an interval in your life, or a single incident. You can shape your auto-biography on a theme or you can try a free-flowing autobiography. But you may *not* include any of the material from your previous autobiography.

THE EXERCISE

DAY: _____   DATE: _____

Allow yourself 5 minutes to decide what you want to write about, and how. Time yourself.

1. Now take 10 minutes and write your autobiography. Again, time yourself. When you've fin-ished (that is, in 10 minutes) answer the questions.

_____

_____

_____

_____

_____

_____

2.   Look back at this second autobiography. How is it different from your first one?

_____

_____

_____

_____

_____

_____

_____

3.   *Why* is this autobiography different?

_____

_____

_____

_____

_____

_____

_____

4.   Would someone reading the two autobiographies realize they were reading about the same person?

_____

_____

_____

_____

_____

_____

_____

5. What influenced your choice of material or style for this autobiography?

_____

_____

_____

_____

_____

_____

_____

_____

PROCESS POINTS

- Could you see differences in the way you presented yourself in the two autobiographies?

- Looking back at the two autobiographies, how are they related? Together, what do they say about you as a person?

- Was it difficult or simple to write this second autobiography? Did you discover anything different about yourself?

The Imaginary Autobiography

Overview

This is yet another version of the 10-minute autobiography, except this auto-biography is more of an exercise in creative writing and creative thinking. In this exercise you'll explore who you are, who you aren't, and who you might like to be.

Instructions

Allot 10 minutes. Write an autobiographical sketch that is entirely imaginative. Create an artificial autobiography in which nothing is true about you. However, write an autobiography that is *believable;* despite being imaginary, don't include details so fantastic as to be unrealistic.

That's it, no further rules or instruction.

THE EXERCISE

DAY: _____   DATE: _____

Allow yourself 5 minutes to decide what you want to write about, and how.

1. Now take 10 minutes and write. When you've finished (that is, in 10 minutes) answer the questions.

_____

_____

_____

_____

_____

_____

_____

_____

_____

2. Even though this autobiography is imaginary, what does your choice of subject matter, style, or the way in which you presented yourself say about you?

_____

_____

_____

_____

_____

_____

_____

_____

_____

_____

3. What influenced your choices in this imaginary autobiography?

_____

_____

_____

_____

_____

_____

_____

_____

_____

_____

_____

4. Would someone who knew you and read this autobiography realize they were reading about you?

_____

_____

_____

_____

_____

_____

_____

_____

_____

_____

_____

_____

5. Might someone who knew you and read this autobiography believe it was true of you?

_____

_____

_____

_____

_____

_____

_____

_____

_____

_____

_____

_____

PROCESS POINTS

- Did it seem foolish to create an imaginary autobiography? Was it difficult or simple to write this imaginary autobiography?

- Looking back at your three autobiographies (two real, one imaginary), how are they related? Together, what do they say about you as you were, are, and hope to be?

Visiting Your Childhood House

Overview

In early childhood, people are often aware of and open to much more than they might be as adults. They can also often remember more from their childhoods than they might realize. This exercise, besides bringing you back to an important time in your life, can help awaken in you the power of observation found in young children but perhaps only rarely used by adults.

This exercise is designed to help you recapture memories through the things you associate with those memories. You will first draw a floor plan of your childhood house, and then a map of your yard and your neighborhood. Next, take someone on a guided tour of the house, yard, and neighborhood. Point out the special memories and special places, comment on the smells or sounds you might associate with parts of your maps, or the toys or people you associate with special places.

This exercise may be difficult for people whose memories of childhood are confusing, stressful, or even frightening. In these cases, you may want to skip this exercise at this time or work on it with someone you trust or who can support you, or with your therapist.

Instructions

1. On a blank sheet of paper, draw the floor plan of your house as best you can. Draw plans of all the floors, including the basement and attic, if you lived in a house with more than one floor.

2. Then draw a plan of the front and back yards, with an outline of the house correctly situated.

3. Finally, draw a map of the immediate neighborhood, starting with the location of your house in the neighborhood.

You may have to take several shots at these drawings, but don't worry about it. For people not used to drawing, it takes a little bit of practice to be comfortable. You may need to practice with the size of your drawings, and you may want to use a ruler to help you with straight lines. Draw in pencil at first, and keep an eraser handy. Remember that the goal of the drawings is not to produce highly skilled artwork, but to create a representation of your house and neighborhood.

4. Once you feel satisfied with your floor plans and maps, walk through them with a friend, a family member, or even someone who lived there with you. Or imagine you are walking a guest through them. In either case, give a tour. Walk through the house, the yard, and the neighborhood. Tell your guest what to look at. Comment on smells. Point out places where special things happened. Tell your guest about special people and memories associated with different places.

THE EXERCISE

1. Draw a floor plan of your house in the space provided.

2. Draw a map of your yard (if you had one). Mark a small square to indicate the position of the house in the yard.

3. Draw a map of your block, or neighborhood. Label neighbors' houses, stores, and streets.

4. Was it easy to remember a past house and surroundings, or difficult? Were you surprised by how much you could remember, or was it difficult to remember the details? Did it become easier to remember details as you progressed?

_____

_____

_____

_____

_____

_____

5. How did you experience this exercise emotionally? Was it difficult, pleasant, sad?

_____

_____

_____

_____

_____

_____

6. Was the process of remembering made easier by conducting the tour itself? Did sharing your memory with someone else enhance your ability to recall detail?

_____

_____

_____

_____

_____

_____

7. Did you find that a lot of your memories were linked to geographic locations, smells, or sounds?

_____

_____

_____

_____

_____

_____

_____

PROCESS POINTS

- Were you surprised at how much you could remember about your old house or neighborhood, or disappointed by how little you remembered?

- Do you want to revisit your old house or neighborhood? If it is possible to take your guest to your old house, what memories would resurface?

In a Child's Voice

Overview

It is difficult for adults to recapture the thinking process or expressive voice of a child. The young child's notions of time, sequence, point of view, and cause and effect are very different from our own.

For most of us, this exercise can only help us to imagine the way a child might think and see the world; nevertheless, it may also help us to recall something about our childhood thought patterns. Where Exercise 31, Visiting Your Childhood House, was designed to help you recollect memories through the things you associated with them, this exercise aims at helping you recapture some of the ways in which you thought about things and saw the world.

Instructions

1. Pick one of the incidents or memories you mentioned while giving your tour in Exercise 31. Do your best to describe the incident as you might have at the time it occurred and at your age then.

2. Write in the present or recent past tense as though the event were happening right now or had just happened moments ago. Use short, or even incomplete sentences. Use small words. Describe without analyzing or evaluating; that is, don't edit what you are writing. Focus on details, memories, and feelings, many of which may seem irrelevant or foolish to you now, as an adult. If you need to, fill in and even make up some of the gaps in your memory. This is an exercise, not an accurate autobiography.

THE EXERCISE

Use the space provided to describe, in a child's voice, a memory or incident recalled by you in Exercise 31, Visiting Your Childhood House.

_____

_____

_____

_____

_____

_____

_____

_____

_____

_____

_____

_____

_____

_____

_____

_____

_____

_____

_____

_____

_____

_____

_____

_____

_____

_____

_____

PROCESS POINTS

- Were you able to think and describe the memory from a child's perspective? If not, why not; what got in the way?

- Did you learn anything about yourself by trying to express yourself in a child's voice? Did the exercise evoke any strong or surprising feelings for you?

Houses, Apartments, and Dormitories

Overview

There is a growing awareness of the importance of location and the effects that place has on individuals. By looking at the various places you have lived, you can become aware of not only how these places have differed from one another, but also how *you* have differed as you moved through your life, marked by the different places you have lived. Thinking about these places gives you an opportunity to understand how they reflect your life at a point in time, and how they may have actually influenced and affected you.

Instructions

Make an inventory of every place you have lived for more than three months, following the directions provided in step 1.

THE EXERCISE

1. To the best of your ability, list every place you have lived for more than three months. Follow this format for each place you list. Briefly describe:
   - Your age
   - What you were doing at that time
   - What you liked about the place you lived
   - What you didn't like about the place you lived
   - How that place somehow marked or reflected that stage in your life

Place 1

Age: _____

What you were doing: _____

What you liked about this place: _____

What you didn't like about this place: _____

How this place reflected your lifestyle: _____

_____

_____

Place 2

Age: _____

What you were doing: _____

What you liked about this place: _____

What you didn't like about this place: _____

How this place reflected your lifestyle: _____

_____

_____

Place 3

Age: _____

What you were doing: _____

What you liked about this place: _____

What you didn't like about this place: _____

How this place reflected your lifestyle: _____

_____

_____

Place 4

Age: _____

What you were doing: _____

What you liked about this place: _____

What you didn't like about this place: _____

How this place reflected your lifestyle: _____

_____

_____

Place 5

Age: _____

What you were doing: _____

What you liked about this place: _____

What you didn't like about this place: _____

How this place reflected your lifestyle: _____

_____

_____

Place 6

Age: _____

What you were doing: _____

What you liked about this place: _____

What you didn't like about this place: _____

How this place reflected your lifestyle: _____

_____

_____

Place 7

Age: _____

What you were doing: _____

What you liked about this place: _____

What you didn't like about this place: _____

How this place reflected your lifestyle: _____

_____

_____

Place 8

Age: _____

What you were doing: _____

What you liked about this place: _____

What you didn't like about this place: _____

How this place reflected your lifestyle: _____

_____

_____

Place 9

Age: _____

What you were doing: _____

What you liked about this place: _____

What you didn't like about this place: _____

How this place reflected your lifestyle: _____

_____

_____

Place 10

Age: _____

What you were doing: _____

What you liked about this place: _____

What you didn't like about this place: _____

How this place reflected your lifestyle: _____

_____

_____

2.   What have you learned about the places you have lived?

_____

_____

_____

_____

_____

_____

3.   What have you learned about yourself from reviewing the places you have lived?

_____

_____

_____

_____

_____

_____

4.   How have the various places you've lived affected your choice of your present living situa-
      tion, the way your current house or apartment looks and is decorated, and the way you
      choose to live?

_____

_____

_____

_____

_____

_____

PROCESS POINTS

- Did you discover anything important about any of the places you lived and their
  effects on your life?

- Did the exercise help you to better understand who you are now, and how you
  came to be that person?

Riding the School Bus

Overview

Many children ride a school bus to and from school. Although there is usually some adult supervision on the buses, some buses and bus rides are chaotic and sometimes frightening rather than pleasant. In this exercise, you'll recollect and describe some of your experiences on the school bus.

Instructions

1. List the schools you have attended.

2. For each school where you rode a bus, describe what you recall about the bus ride. Try to recall the bus number, the name of the driver and other adult supervisors on the bus, the other students you sat with, and so on, and then describe your emotional experience on the bus: was it pleasant, confusing, frightening, safe?

3. Finally, explain how that bus journey affected or reflected your life in and outside of school at that time.

THE EXERCISE

To the best of your ability list every school you attended using the following format for each school on your list. Briefly describe:

- Your age and the school you attended at the time

- Details of the school bus itself: bus number, driver, other adult supervision on the bus

- Where the bus picked you up

- Other students who rode the bus and were of importance to you, for any reason (good or bad)

- The emotional nature of your experience on the bus: good, bad, scary, safe, etc.

- If the bus journey somehow set the tone for that day in school, and how your reactions to the journey reflected or affected your life at that time.

Bus 1

age/school attended: _____

bus #/driver/adults: _____

where the bus picked you up: _____

important students who rode the bus: _____

emotional experience on the bus: _____

impact on your daily life: _____

_____

_____

_____

_____

_____

Bus 2

age/school attended: _____

bus #/driver/adults: _____

where the bus picked you up: _____

important students who rode the bus: _____

emotional experience on the bus: _____

impact on your daily life: _____

_____

_____

_____

_____

_____

Bus 3

age/school attended: _____

bus #/driver/adults: _____

where the bus picked you up: _____

important students who rode the bus: _____

emotional experience on the bus: _____

impact on your daily life: _____

_____

_____

_____

_____

_____

Bus 4

age/school attended: _____

bus #/driver/adults: _____

where the bus picked you up: _____

important students who rode the bus: _____

emotional experience on the bus: _____

impact on your daily life: _____

_____

_____

_____

_____

Bus 5

age/school attended: _____

bus #/driver/adults: _____

where the bus picked you up: _____

important students who rode the bus: _____

emotional experience on the bus: _____

impact on your daily life: _____

_____

_____

_____

_____

_____

Bus 6

age/school attended: _____

bus #/driver/adults: _____

where the bus picked you up: _____

important students who rode the bus: _____

emotional experience on the bus: _____

impact on your daily life: _____

_____

_____

_____

_____

_____

PROCESS POINTS

- Has recalling school bus journeys helped you to remember details of your life and feelings during your childhood?

- Do your school bus experiences reflect the way you generally recall your life at those times?

- Did your school bus experiences affect the way you have come to see yourself and others? How?

SECTION IV

Review

- In Section IV you reviewed important people, places, and events in your life. Each exercise focused on a particular part of your life. Now take a minute to reflect on your overall history.

- If you were to divide your life into phases or epochs, what would they be?

- Do you see your life as a steady progression, a series of random events, or a combination of times of emotional stability and times of change?

- If your life seems to be a mixture of steady times and change times, which are you in now?

- Before going on to Section V, take a minute to review and renew your commitment to this process.

SECTION

Charting Your Future: Finding Solutions and Solving Problems

EXERCISE **35**

Creating an
Awareness Log

Overview

It is possible to use a journal like a record—a log—of specific experiences and reactions. In this way, journal entries can help you to pinpoint your feelings about or reactions to an event, precursors or precipitants to a problem or emotional/physical difficulty, or in some way help you to maintain an accurate record about what happened when, why, how, and in what order.

For instance, if you get depressed it can help to log how you were feeling before you got depressed, what happened right before you became depressed or led to your becoming depressed, and what happened right after. Logs like this can help you to make sense of your behavior, moods, experiences, and reactions.

You can use a log to track:

- Feelings—such as depression, anxiety, and anger or joy, excitement, and contentment

- Behaviors—such as impulsive reactions, self-destructive actions, productivity, and responsibility

- Bodily states—such as migraine headaches, substance cravings, high energy, or physical well-being

Remember that the point of the log is to help you capture the events leading up to, during, and after the experience. The point is to help you to understand yourself a little better and the environmental causes of your feelings or behaviors.

Instructions

1. Pick your target feelings, behaviors, or states.

2. Write the target on the log.

3. Photocopy the log and use it to track the onset of the feeling, behavior, or state over a 1-week period.

4. Analyze the commonalities.

THE EXERCISE

_____ **AWARENESS LOG**

DAY: _____   DATE: _____

1. Did you feel _____ today: Yes   No

2. Was the feeling, behavior, or bodily state:

    Continuous

    Intermittent during the day

    A single occurrence (how long did it last): _____

3. What time did the feeling, behavior, or bodily state first begin? _____

4. How strong was the experience at its most extreme (circle)?

pretty mild		_moderate_			_very strong_	

        1   2   3   4   5   6   7   8   9   10

5. What other feelings or symptoms accompanied the feeling, behavior, or bodily state?

___ depression	___ anxiety/worry	___ peacefulness
___ fear	___ irritation	___ joy
___ anger	___ sadness	___ contentment
___ racing thoughts	___ confusion	___ satisfaction
___ frustration	___ tension	___ clarity

    Other: _____

6. What feelings can you remember just before you experienced the feeling, behavior, or bodily state?

    _____

    _____

    _____

7. What activities or events took place just before the onset of the feeling, behavior, or bodily state?

    _____

    _____

    _____

8. What were you thinking about just before the onset of the feeling, behavior, or bodily state?

_____

_____

_____

_____

9. Why do you think you experienced the feeling, behavior, or bodily state?

_____

_____

_____

_____

_____

_____

10. What did you do to relieve or sustain the feeling, behavior, or bodily state?

_____

_____

_____

_____

_____

11. Did it work?

_____

_____

12. What did you do after the event?

_____

_____

_____

_____

13. Do you understand why you experienced the feeling, behavior, or bodily state?

_____

_____

14. In the event of a negative experience, what can you do to avoid, reduce, or relieve the feeling, behavior, or bodily state in the future? In the event of a positive experience, what can you do to generate, renew, or prolong the feeling, behavior, or bodily state in the future?

_____

_____

_____

_____

_____

_____

_____

PROCESS POINTS
- Did the charting process help you to better understand yourself and your life?
- Are there specific areas in your life (e.g., feelings, behaviors, or bodily states) that charting will help you to better understand, predict, and/or control?

Opposites

Overview

It is easy to see the world in black or white. Shades of gray are harder to accept.

"Dialectics" is the art of creation through the resolution of opposites. It is a process in which the contradiction between one idea (the *thesis*) and its opposite idea (the *antithesis*) is resolved by blending the two ideas together (*synthesis*), thus forming a new reality. Dialectics is not the art of compromise (a primary skill in the world of relationships); it is the art of creating new ideas from opposites.

And from every new idea (the thesis) comes yet another opposite idea (its antithesis): the synthesis (coming together) of opposing ideas leads directly to another round of opposites. In a way, dialectics is built on the idea that contradiction naturally exists in the world and continually tries to seek resolution to seemingly unresolvable differences.

Instructions

Think of a situation or an idea in which you see a conflict. It may be a situation in which you are involved, an argument, a political belief, or another circumstance in which you believe you are correct or a particular idea is correct. Pick a situation in which there is an obvious opposite point of view.

1. Briefly describe the situation you have selected for this exercise. The idea is not to explore the situation giving rise to the conflict, but ways to resolve the seeming contradictions that arise as the result of one idea or another.

2. Describe the *essential* question to be resolved. What is at the heart of the conflict of ideas?

3. Describe the opposites: name the idea and the opposite idea.

4. Explore both the idea and the opposite idea. Use short sentences to list the elements of each.

5. Describe the basic issues a little more, in brief sentences.

6. Describe the opposites, and briefly explore the effects of the contradiction.

7. What do you want as an outcome? What you want will influence how much effort you put into finding a resolution to the conflict between ideas.

8. Based on what you want as an outcome, what is the correct goal to work toward to achieve resolution?

9. State that goal in terms of a new idea.

10. And, because this is an exercise, reframe that new idea as the thesis against which you find an *antithesis*. As opposites are not always perfectly clear in the complications of real life, you may have to really think about what actually represents an opposite idea in this case.

Example

1. *The situation:* I got into an argument with my partner, who told me I never listen when he or she speaks. I said of course I listen, it's just that I don't always agree with my partner, who takes my lack of agreement as a sign that I don't listen. Nevertheless, the issue exists that my partner feels I don't listen and this is standing between us.

2. *The essential question:* Do I listen?

3. *The contradiction:* "I listen well" (the thesis) versus "I don't listen well" (the antithesis).

4. *Exploring the opposites.*

Idea	Opposite Idea
I listen	I don't listen
Listening means . . . (to be completed fully in an actual situation)	Not listening means . . . (to be completed fully in an actual situation)
I know I listen because . . . (to be completed fully in an actual situation)	I know I don't listen because . . . (to be completed fully in an actual situation)
There is evidence that I do listen	There is evidence that I don't listen
Do I listen?	Do I not listen?
It's unfair for my partner to criticize my listening skills	It's legitimate for my partner to criticize my listening skills
I can't improve my listening skills	I can improve my listening skills
I shouldn't have to improve my listening skills	I should have to improve my listening skills

5. *What are the issues:*
   - Does my partner feel I don't listen well enough?
   - Does it hurt to be criticized or misunderstood?
   - Can I overcome the feelings raised by this issue?
   - Are my feelings preventing me from finding solutions or making changes?

- Do I want to improve my relationship with my partner?
- Do I want to improve my listening skills?
- What will happen if the situation doesn't improve?

6. *The nature of the contradiction and its effects:*   The opposites in this care are "my listening skills are fine as they are and *shouldn't* affect my relationship with my partner" versus "my listening skills are not fine as they are and *should* affect my relationship with my partner." The outcome—or the resolution to this contradiction—will be built on what I most want in this case.

7. *What do I want in this situation:*   In this case, the problem of listening versus *not* listening is interfering with my relationship with my partner, and I do want that relationship to improve.

8. *Resolving the contradiction:*   Whether my listening skills are good or not, the issue is affecting my relationship. In this case, the synthesis becomes "I ought to work on improving my listening skills as this will help to improve my relationship."

9. *The new idea:*   I ought to work on improving my listening skills.

10. *The new opposite idea:*   In this exercise, we go to the next level of the dialectic. That is, *every* idea has an opposite idea including the newly synthesized idea. In fact, the synthesis merely provides the starting point for a new round of resolution. In this case, the new idea is "I will work on improving my listening skills." The opposite idea that I have chosen (remember that opposites are not always as clear as hot and cold and there may be many choices) is "I shouldn't *have* to change to suit my partner's needs; my partner should accept me as I am."

THE EXERCISE

1. The situation:

_____

_____

_____

_____

_____

2. The essential question:

_____

_____

3. The contradiction:

    The idea: _____

    The opposite idea: _____

4. Exploring the opposites:

The idea	*The opposite idea*
_____	_____
_____	_____
_____	_____
_____	_____
_____	_____
_____	_____
_____	_____
_____	_____

5. What are the issues:

    _____

    _____

    _____

    _____

    _____

    _____

6. The nature of the contradiction and its effects:

    _____

    _____

    _____

    _____

    _____

    _____

7. What do I want in this situation:

_____

_____

_____

_____

8. Resolving the contradiction:

_____

_____

_____

_____

9. The new idea:

_____

_____

_____

10. The new opposite idea:

_____

_____

_____

_____

PROCESS POINTS

- Do you normally find it difficult to resolve contradiction in your life?
- Did this exercise help you to see contradiction in a different way?
- Were you able to find a meaningful way to resolve the contradiction you selected for this exercise?

Irrational Thinking and Behavior: A Self-Defeating Cycle

Overview

People often do not behave rationally. That is, the things they do (or their *behavior*) in a given situation aren't necessarily the rational things to do in that particular situation. Irrational behavior is usually shaped by irrational *thinking*.

How we feel and how we think affect our behavior. Exercise 38, "Cause and Effect," helps you to connect your feelings to your thoughts, and your thoughts to your behavior. Complete Exercise 38 after you've finished this exercise.

If you believe that your feelings and thoughts influence and shape your behavior, then you understand that you can get into a self-defeating and self-perpetuating *cycle* of behaviors in which: (1) A difficult situation can lead to . . . (2) unpleasant feelings that can lead to . . . (3) behavior that can have . . . (4) unpleasant and difficult consequences that lead back to . . . (5) a difficult situation.

You can break this cycle by looking at your response to situations and changing your *irrational* thoughts and beliefs to thoughts and beliefs that are more *rational* and *realistic*.

Common Patterns of Irrational Thinking

1. *Emotional misreasoning.* You draw an irrational and incorrect conclusion based on the way you feel at that moment: I *feel* this way, therefore I *am* this way. I *feel* like a piece of garbage, so I must *be* a piece of garbage.

2. *Overgeneralization.* You draw an incorrect conclusion that has far-reaching implications based on a single experience or a small set of experiences: I failed to do well in *this* particular situation, so I must be a failure in *all* situations.

3. *Catastrophic thinking.* An extreme example of overgeneralization, in which you magnify the impact of a negative experience to extreme proportions: If I have a panic attack, I will lose *all* control and go crazy, or die.

4. *Black-and-white (either/or) thinking.* You simplistically divide complex situations into opposite (*polarized*) extremes: *Either* I am a success at this, *or* I am a total failure. *If* I'm not perfect, *then* I must be imperfect.

5. *Shoulds and musts.* You feel that you absolutely *must* behave in a particular way or think that you *should* have a level of control over the world around you: I *should* be better at this than I am. I *must* complete this task.

6. *Negative predictions (fortune-telling).* You predict failure for yourself in a new situation because you experienced failure in an earlier situation: I have not done well in these situations in the *past,* and therefore I will *never* do well in these situations.

7. *Projection.* You make negative assumptions about the thoughts, intentions, or motives of another person: She doesn't like the way I look. She thinks I'm a loser. He thinks I'm a fool.

8. *Mind reading.* You think that other people *ought* to know how you feel, or what you want, even though you haven't told them: He *ought* to know that I don't like that kind of chocolate. She *ought* to know I don't like it when she does that.

9. *Labeling.* You make an undesirable characteristic of yourself or another person *definitive* for simplistic reasons: Because I failed to be selected for ballet, I *am* a failure. Because he didn't listen to me, he *is* unsupportive.

10. *Personalization.* You treat a negative event as a personal reflection or confirmation of your own worthlessness: Because I wasn't selected for *that* job, I *am* a failure—as I knew anyway. Nothing ever goes right for me because I'm worthless.

11. *Negative focus.* You focus on negative events, memories, or implications while you ignore or even disqualify more neutral or positive information about yourself or a situation: It *doesn't matter* that I have two children who care for and love me or that I have been successful in my job; I'm no good and a failure *because* I didn't do well in that test.

12. *Cognitive avoidance.* Because you don't want to deal with difficult emotions, you interpret unpleasant thoughts, feelings, or events as overwhelming or insurmountable and actively avoid thinking about them further: I can't even *think* about it, let alone try to understand and change it.

13. *Somatic misunderstanding.* You interpret the way your body feels (for example, heart rate, palpitations, shortness of breath, dizziness, or tingling) as a *definite* indication that something bad is about to happen (for example, heart attack, suffocation, or collapse): I *feel* awful, therefore something really bad *must* be about to happen.

Instructions

Referring to the list above, complete the worksheet.

THE EXERCISE

DAY: _____   DATE: _____

1. Look back on today and yesterday. Look back over the past week. Think of situations you
    came away from feeling that you had messed up, or had been cheated or misunderstood by
    someone. Then identify from the following list the general patterns of irrational thought to
    which you are prone (check all that apply):

    ____ *Emotional misreasoning.*   You reach a conclusion or inference based on the way
    you feel, rather than on actual evidence.

    ____ *Overgeneralization.*   You assume that your experience in one situation is a re-
    flection of the ways things are in all situations.

    ____ *Catastrophic thinking.*   You magnify the impact of one negative experience to
    extreme proportions.

    ____ *Black-and-white thinking.*   You see things as all or nothing, either all one way
    or all the other.

    ____ *Shoulds and musts.*   You feel you *should* do something or things *must* be a cer-
    tain way without evidence that your feelings about the situation are correct.

    ____ *Negative predictions/fortune-telling.*   You predict failure in a new situation,
    because things have gone wrong before.

    ____ *Projection.*   You make negative assumptions about the thoughts, intentions, or
    motives of another.

    ____ *Mind reading.*   You feel that others *should* have known how you felt or what you
    wanted even though you didn't tell them.

    ____ *Labeling.*   You label yourself or someone else in a negative way for simplistic
    reasons.

    ____ *Personalization.*   You treat a negative event as a personal reflection or confir-
    mation of your own worthlessness.

    ____ *Negative focus.*   You focus mainly on negative events, memories, or implications
    while you ignore or disqualify more neutral or positive information about your-
    self or a situation.

    ____ *Cognitive avoidance.*   You avoid thinking about emotionally difficult subjects
    because they feel overwhelming or insurmountable.

    ____ *Somatic misunderstanding.*   You misinterpret some pain or some negative sen-
    sation in your body as a sign that something is seriously wrong or is about to go
    seriously wrong.

2. Now try and hone in on particular patterns of irrational thought. Think of a specific situation that was disturbing to you in some way. Briefly describe it.

_____

_____

_____

_____

3. How did you feel during and after the situation?

_____

_____

_____

_____

4. How did you behave during and after the situation?

_____

_____

_____

_____

5. In that situation, how many of the following types of irrational thoughts could be applied to you.

____ Emotional misreasoning

____ Overgeneralization

____ Catastrophic thinking

____ Black and white thinking

____ Shoulds and musts

____ Negative predictions/fortune-telling

____ Projection

____ Mind reading

____ Labeling

____ Personalization

____ Negative focus

____ Cognitive avoidance

____ Somatic misunderstanding

6. Looking over your answers to the checklist above, do you think that the way you *felt* had something to do with the way you were thinking about the situation? In what ways might your *feelings* have been influenced by irrational thinking?

_____

_____

_____

_____

_____

7. Looking over your answers to the preceding checklist, do you think that the way you *behaved* had something to do with the way you were thinking about the situation? In what ways might your behaviors have been influenced by irrational thinking?

_____

_____

_____

_____

_____

_____

_____

PROCESS POINTS

- Are your patterns of thinking irrational at times and do they shape the way you see yourself in the world at certain times or under certain conditions?

- In what ways might you find different, more rational ways to think about situations?

Cause and Effect—
Situations and Behaviors

Overview

Things that happen in your environment affect and shape your behavior. There is a cause-and-effect relationship between situations and behaviors: (1) First something happens—the *situation;* (2) you have a particular response to what happened—your *feelings;* (3) you analyze your feelings in light of your life experiences—your feelings lead to your thoughts, and (4) your thoughts lead to decisions about how to respond to the situation—your *behavior.*

This exercise provides a way for you to connect situations to behaviors, and to reflect on the links between feelings and thoughts.

Instructions

Use the following chart to trace what happened to you and your eventual behavior. You can use the chart to describe almost any situation and its outcome—that is, your behavior.

1. In the Description column, simply describe:

    *   What *happened*—the situation.   Describe anything from an event to something someone said to you.

    *   How you *felt*—your feelings.   After the situation or event took place, how did you feel? Were you hurt, upset, angry, happy, etc.?

    *   How you *intellectually reacted*—your thoughts.   What thoughts followed your feelings? Did you feel that you had been insulted, misunderstood, complimented, attacked, etc.?

    *   What you did you *do*—your behavior.   Did you yell at someone, cry, run away, give someone a hug, curl up in a ball, hurt yourself, hurt someone else, etc.?

    It can be hard to separate feelings from thoughts, and many times people confuse the two. Try to distinguish the *emotional* process of feeling, from the *intellectual* process of thinking.

2. In the Evaluation column, describe the situation, your feelings, your thoughts, and your behaviors from an objective point of view. That is, looking back on the situation, how would someone else see it—do you see it differently?

    If you completed Exercise 37, you'll remember that there are different patterns and types of irrational thinking. Were your thoughts that followed your feelings rational, or were they an irrational response to the initiating situation? Was your behavior a suitable, appropriate, or productive response to the initiating situation?

3. In the Review area below the chart, describe what went wrong in the connection(s) between the original situation and your eventual behavior. How would you do things differently in the same situation? How can you change things from here on?

Example

	Description	Evaluation
Situation	I enrolled in an evening business course leading to a professional degree. During my second class, the instructor called on me to answer a question, but I couldn't because the terminology was still unfamiliar to me. I noticed that several others in the class seemed able to come up with answers, though.	I understandably felt out of place in this new environment. I let the concerns I brought in with me and my general lack of confidence get the better of me as soon as something didn't go quite right.
Feeling	I felt like a complete idiot. I felt embarrassed and humiliated and a whole lot more stupid than everyone else in the class.	Most students didn't volunteer to answer questions, and other people couldn't answer when called on. Only a few students could answer the professor, and she didn't seem to mind when answers were wrong.
Thought	I thought that I shouldn't be in this class, that I'm too old to go back to school. I thought that I don't have the intellectual or academic skills to retrain myself, and I thought I'd never be able to complete the course.	Probably a lot of people in the class were feeling this way, with the possible exception of the few students who had taken business courses before and were just out of undergraduate school.
Behavior	I didn't talk much to my husband or kids when I got home and was reclusive for the rest of the night. At work the next day, I remained distant from people. The following day, I decided to cut the class and later that week officially withdrew from the course.	I didn't take the time to discuss my feelings and self-doubts with anyone, including close friends. I let my insecurities get the better of me and simply escaped the situation without waiting to see how I felt after several more classes. My quitting only lowered my self-esteem further.

1. What went wrong in terms of the progression between the situations, your feelings, your thoughts, and your behaviors?

   I let my self-doubt immediately get in my way. As soon as things seemed to go wrong, I panicked. Things didn't actually go wrong—I was simply unable to answer a question because the course work was so new to me. But I overreacted and let that initial situation get to me. I started obsessing on it and eventually behaved in a way that further undermined my self-confidence by quitting a project that I really wanted to complete.

2. How could you behave differently in the same situation?

   I shouldn't expect to achieve success all at once. Without lowering my expectations of myself, I could be more realistic about what I can do as I develop new skills. I could talk to my friends and get their support and reassurance. I could even discuss my concerns with the professor. I certainly shouldn't let my feelings run away with me and control my behaviors.

THE EXERCISE

DAY: _____   DATE: _____

	Description	**Evaluation**
Situation		
Feeling		

	Description	Evaluation
Thought		
Behavior		

1. What went wrong in terms of the progression between the situations, your feelings, your thoughts, and your behaviors?

_____

_____

_____

_____

_____

_____

_____

_____

_____

_____

2. How could you behave differently in the same situation?

_____

_____

_____

_____

_____

_____

_____

_____

_____

_____

PROCESS POINTS

- Was it useful to consider your behavior as part of a cycle of events that runs from situation to behavior?

- Do you want to take more control over your emotions and interrupt this situation-behavior cycle to make more rational decisions in your life? Are there situations where you'd rather simply let your feelings shape your behaviors without having to exercise rational thought?

- Can you recognize the difference between situations where you want your emotions to rule your behaviors and situations where you want your intellect to shape your behaviors?

EXERCISE

Understanding Your Goals

Overview

Goals are complicated. They sound so simple, yet often demand a great deal of energy and commitment. Because people often underestimate the complexity of setting goals, they may not achieve the ends they seek. Before your goals can be accomplished, you need to articulate exactly what the goals are.

Instructions

Think of a goal you'd like to achieve. Answer the questions below.

THE EXERCISE

1. What is my goal?

_____

_____

2. What *exactly* do I want to achieve?

_____

_____

_____

3. Why do I want this?

_____

_____

_____

4. How am I going to achieve my goal?

_____

_____

_____

_____

5. What will happen if I achieve my goal?

_____

_____

_____

_____

6. What will happen if I don't achieve my goal?

_____

_____

_____

_____

7. What obstacles will I have to overcome to achieve this goal?

_____

_____

_____

_____

8. Am I really committed to achieving this goal?

_____

_____

_____

_____

9. Of all the goals and priorities in my life, how important is this goal to me on a 1–5 scale?
    1 = least important and 10 = most important

                    1   2   3   4   5

PROCESS POINTS
- Did the exercise help you to clarify the meaning of goals in general?
- Did the exercise help you to clarify the meaning of this particular goal to you? Do you understand the value of this goal to you? Do you understand the kind of problems you might face in trying to achieve this goal?

Achieving Your Goals

Overview

You identified a goal in Exercise 39, "Understanding Your Goals." Now take a closer look at that same goal and its subgoals—the partial objectives and activities that must be undertaken and completed to achieve the goal.

This exercise can help you to make sense of your goals, and perhaps more important, to focus on what you must *do* to achieve your goals. When you explore the goal-setting process, you may discover things about yourself, your skills, and your personal obstacles to goal achievement.

Instructions

1. *Pick a goal (level A).*   Goals are usually described in very broad and abstract terms, such as "I want to quit smoking," "I want to be more successful in business this year," or "I want to improve my relationships with others." In these cases the goal is clear, but the obstacles to goal achievement, or the smaller goals (subgoals) that must first be achieved to reach the main goal, are pretty vague.

2. *Identify component subgoals (level B).*   For instance, saying "I want to improve my relationships" can be broken down further into several smaller goals (subgoals) that are far more *specific,* such as:

   • "I want to improve my relationship with my spouse."

   • "I want to improve my relationship with my family."

   • "I want to improve my relationship with colleagues at work."

3. *Identify microgoals (level C).*   The list of subgoals can often be broken down into an even more specific set of microgoals. That is, in what ways do you want to improve your relationships with these various groups of people? As the microgoals get developed at these more specific levels, they become increasingly more defined and detailed. Improving your relationship with your spouse might include:

   • Improving your sexual relationship

   • Improving your ability to simply converse

   • Focusing on your relationship as parents to a shared child

   Fulfill your microgoals—and the larger goals will follow.

Example

In this example we provide three levels of goals: the broad goal (level A), subgoals (level B) that are derived from the broad goal, and microgoals (level C) that are drawn from the level B goals. Notice that each lower-level set of goals becomes more *specific* and more *measurable*.

You could go on forever of course, adding level after level of sub- or microgoals, but this would soon get ridiculous. Three levels is usually plenty to really define and understand what is required to achieve your broad goal. The last level of goals is the most specific and leads directly to the actual activities you must engage in to complete and achieve your goals. Achieving *all* the sub- and microgoals at lower levels automatically fulfills the requirements for goal achievement at the next highest level.

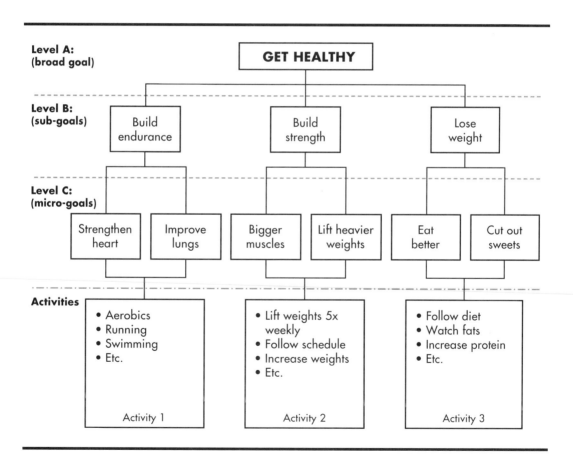

THE EXERCISE

In this exercise, using our example as a model, you'll define three levels of goals: your broad goal (level A) and, beneath that, subgoals and microgoals (levels B and C) and a related set of goal activities.

You can use the blank flow chart included here to build your own set of goals, subgoals, and activities as we did in our example.

You can also use the more complex worksheet that follows to work through each goal, subgoal, and microgoal, and to define the activities you'll need to undertake to achieve them.

Use the goal you said you wanted to achieve in Exercise 39 as your level A broad goal.

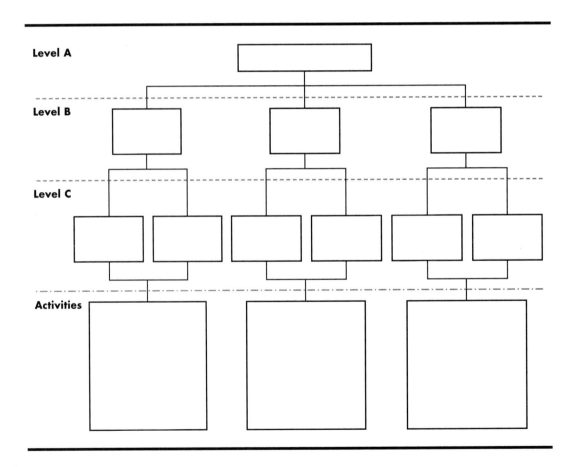

GOAL SETTING WORKSHEET

1. Once again describe the goal you said you wanted to achieve in Exercise 39. This is your *first level* broad goal (level A).

    _____

2. Now go to your *second level* subgoals (level B): Further define your broad goal by naming the more specific goals that you will need to accomplish at this second level. Name three level B subgoals, as we did in our example.

    a) _____

    b) _____

    c) _____

3. Take the first level B subgoal (subgoal *a* above) and write it in here:

    a) _____

    Now develop two level C microgoals for subgoal *a.*

    a (1) _____

    a (2) _____

    Take the second level B subgoal (subgoal *b* above) and write it in here:

    b) _____

    Now develop two level C microgoals for subgoal *b.*

    b (1) _____

    b (2) _____

    Take the third level B subgoal (subgoal *c* above) and write it in here:

    c) _____

    Now, develop two level C microgoals for subgoal *c.*

    c (1) _____

    c (2) _____

   You now have one broad goal (level A), three subgoals (level B), and six microgoals (level C). As you moved from level A to level C, your goals should have become more specific and more measurable.

4. Now describe the activities you will have to engage in to meet your level C microgoals. If you can, name at least three activities for each level C microgoal.

Activities required to achieve microgoal: *a* (1)

_____

_____

_____

Activities required to achieve microgoal: *a* (2)

_____

_____

_____

Activities required to achieve microgoal: *b* (1)

_____

_____

_____

Activities required to achieve microgoal: *b* (2)

_____

_____

_____

Activities required to achieve microgoal: *c* (1)

_____

_____

_____

Activities required to achieve microgoal: *c* (2)

_____

_____

_____

Complex, isn't it? But if you've completed this worksheet and this exercise, then you've managed to break down a goal into its various component parts, including the things you must *actually* do to achieve the goal.

PROCESS POINTS

- Did the exercise help you to break down the goal-setting process into its various pieces? Has the exercise helped you to understand how to define your goals, and how to go about achieving them?

- What have you learned from this exercise about your *present* method of goal selection and achievement?

SECTION V

Review

- Section V is about taking control of your decision-making and problem-solving skills. Did it help you to think about the way you currently understand, tackle, and resolve life issues? What sort of conclusions did you reach about yourself?

- Has this section helped you to better understand how you see the world and how you process what goes on around you and inside you in response to your environment? Do you better understand the connection between your feelings, your thoughts, and your behaviors?

- What will stop you from using or adapting what you've learned in Section V in your everyday life?

Conclusion

EVERY END IS A NEW BEGINNING

You've reached the end of this long journey. Congratulations, because this means you've fulfilled the promise you made to yourself way back in Exercise 1.

By now, you've learned a number of new skills or further refined some existing ones. You've learned to view yourself from the inside and the outside, you've learned to view the world around you, and you've learned about the connections between your inside world and the environment in which you exist. You've learned the skill of self-examination and analysis: You've stopped to examine yourself and what makes you tick, and you've learned how to step outside of yourself and evaluate your moods and your behaviors. You've learned how to rationally monitor yourself and understand the impact of both the past and the present on who you are, and how and why you think the way you think and do the things you do.

You've learned to put your thoughts into writing, and *how* to put your thoughts into writing. You've acquired the skill of thinking things through and making connections. You've learned to talk to yourself and see your many sides, and you've learned that almost everything has many sides and aspects—just as you do.

This book, then, is entirely about *you*. When it was a book of blank exercises, it was simply an empty shell. Now that it's complete, it's a pure reflection of you.

In completing this book you've accomplished a great deal and taken important and significant steps down the path to self-discovery and healing. Your self-view and self-journey will likely never be complete, but the techniques and lessons learned in this book will help you move further along that path as you seek to complete your journey.

LOOKING BACK

- Now that you've finished the entire workbook, will you be able to maintain the lessons learned and commit yourself to putting them into practice in your everyday life?

- Will you continue to maintain a journal? Will you use a journal for your daily life, or only on occasion to help you sort out a difficult, complex, or trying situation?

- What sort of a journal will you keep? Will it be a series of free-form entries, or will you select some of the exercises from *The Healing Journey* and keep a journal of more structured and formatted entries?

- What will stop you from keeping a journal or remembering the lessons you learned while keeping this journal? What will help you to keep the journaling experience alive and fresh in your mind?

- Where will you travel next on your own healing journey, and what tools or people will you need to help take you further along your path?

ABOUT THE AUTHORS

PHIL RICH, EDD, MSW, holds a doctorate in applied behavioral and organizational studies and is a clinical social worker diplomate with a masters in social work. Over the past two decades, he has worked as a director of treatment programs, clinical supervisor, and a practicing therapist. He is currently actively involved with inpatient care at the Brattleboro Retreat, and maintains a private outpatient practice in western Massachusetts.

STUART A. COPANS, MD, is a board certified child psychiatrist and an associate professor of clinical psychiatry at Dartmouth Medical School. He has practiced child psychiatry at the Brattleboro Retreat for the past 20 years and is also the author of numerous books on psychotherapy and adolescent substance abuse. Dr. Copans is trained in art therapy and frequently makes use of both written and graphic assignments in his work with patients.

Things I like

- Candle light
- Soft clothes
- Roomy shorts
- Quiet
- Birds in flight
- Small pens
- Good champagne
- To see Richard happy on Role
- To feel exhausted
- To have someone open their heart to me
- To be silly with someone   =   Suzzy
                                        Sharon
                                        Marti
                                        Kent
                                        Marti
                                        Bill
                                        Lucy
                                        Beth